Bringing Out the Giftedness in Your Child

Bringing Out the Giftedness in Your Child

Nurturing Every Child's Unique Strengths, Talents, and Potential

Rita Dunn, Ed.D.
Kenneth Dunn, Ed.D.
Donald Treffinger, Ph.D.

John Wiley & Sons, Inc.
New York • Chichester • Brisbane • Toronto • Singapore

Library of Congress Cataloging-in-Publication Data

Dunn, Rita, 1930-
     Bringing out the giftedness in your child: unlocking every child's unique
  strengths, talents, and potential/Rita Dunn, Kenneth Dunn, Donald
  Treffinger.
        p.   cm.
     Includes bibliographical references.
     ISBN 0-471-52803-X
     1. Child development—United States.   2. Achievement motivation in
  children.   3. Child rearing—United States.   4. Learning.   I. Dunn,
  Kenneth.   II. Treffinger, Donald J.   III. Title.
  HQ792.U5D86   1991
  305.23′1—dc20   91-13185

Printed and bound by Courier Companies, Inc.

This book is dedicated to our beloved children:
Rana, Robert, Richard, Kerry, Kevin, and Keith Dunn
and
Ken Treffinger and Judy Treffinger Ackerman,
and our grandchildren:
Ryan Dunn Mosler
and
Ashley and Tyler Ackerman—
each of whom has developed unique individual gifts!

Preface

Every parent knows that each child is different from every other. It is unusual to be able to rear two children in the same way; what works for one, rarely does for another. Parents often believe that they must treat each youngster identically; that is untrue. There is nothing so unequal as the equal treatment of unequals. All children are valuable and worthy, but each has different potentials which, if nurtured and encouraged, develop into strengths, talents, and, ultimately, gifts. Each person's potentials are very different from everyone else's; in the same family, the mother, father, siblings, and relatives are likely to shine in special ways that are unique to them.

Unfortunately, society, schools, and books on parenting do not prepare us to rear our offspring in ways that develop their *individual* potentials. Children in the same family often are required to engage in identical routines and patterns or to participate in essentially similar activities. Parents then see one child thrive and others either merely survive in very ordinary ways or become nonconforming; many children do not reach levels of achievement we believed possible.

This book is intended to overcome the age-old belief that children are born with giftedness. To the contrary, we believe that the natural talents that lie within every human being can be nurtured through activities and opportunities presented at home, in school, and in the total environment. When children appreciate their own potentials and become interested in anything that stimulates their minds, bodies, emotions, or psyches, *they* plunge into further exploration and, eventually, their individual strengths and talents *become* their giftedness.

We designed the book to bring joy and positive feelings to parents and all adults who live or work with children. Our broad, yet practical view of giftedness and individual strengths includes definitions and descriptions that will make recognition of *every* child's potentials and talents easy and exciting. If you try the simple-to-follow advice and activities, you will build confidence in the youngsters with whom you come into contact and, eventually, will marvel at their successes.

For example, did you realize that the typical intelligence quotient (IQ) test measures only about 10 to 15 percent of all known aspects of intellectual ability? In Chapter 1, we describe different kinds of intelligence and explain our focus. Next, we provide questions, ways of observing, and practical suggestions for recognizing your child's potentials and talents. Chapter 2 presents the basis of our beliefs in individual differences and strengths and discusses the notion that individual learning style is the single most important factor in developing a child's giftedness. The illustrations in the chapter were adapted from materials provided by the Orchard Park Central School, Orchard Park, New York.

How can you use your apartment or home, and everything that is available there, to nurture your child's potential from birth through the school years? Which teachers' teaching style best matches your youngsters' learning style strengths? Why should you pressure your child's school principal for the best possible student–teacher instructional match? Because one year of "lost" schooling is rarely regained, and "turning off" a child is exactly what must *not* happen!

Later chapters reveal practical steps you can take to increase your child's interests and productivity. We describe methods to improve children's ability to think creatively, solve problems, and make decisions, and we detail ways to assist them in becoming independent learners. You will find many practical suggestions throughout the text and a collection of resources in the appendices. We hope you will share with us the belief that giftedness is a potential that is not limited to a few children who have a narrow range of talents. When nurtured through support of each individual's learning style, giftedness emerges and blooms. We wish you successful, healthy, happy children whose strengths and talents are nurtured to levels beyond your own expectations.

RITA AND KEN DUNN
DONALD TREFFINGER

Pound Ridge, New York
Sarasota, Florida
December 1991

Contents

Bringing Out
the Giftedness
in Your Child

1

How Is Your Child Gifted?

Many books and magazine articles describe "the gifted child" and tell parents how to recognize one. Telltale signs of giftedness, often different in each publication, are listed so that budding geniuses won't be missed or their development stifled. When did your child learn to crawl? How early was your child potty trained? Did your baby gurgle in unusual ways or demonstrate exceptional agility with a teddy bear? Be alert! You may have a gifted child.

Child-care professionals receive hundreds of calls every year from eager (or terrified) parents who have "discovered" from their reading that they have a gifted child. For some parents, the discovery is cause for considerable fear. They may even apologize: "We don't know how this could have happened. Certainly nothing like this has ever happened in our family before." For other parents, eager to have a proof of their own giftedness, their child's superior talents are only to be expected. Whether forecast to be a burden or an intellectual and social status symbol, the gifted child is seen to be someone rare and unusual.

Our book approaches a child's gifts from a different point of view. We don't rely on the narrow, traditional definition of "the gifted child" or the pseudo-official phrase parroted by

1

many parents, "the identified gifted child." Our book deals with finding and nurturing the gifts—the opportunities for accomplishment and creativity—in every child.

Our Definition of Giftedness

Giftedness should extend far beyond a category or label; it should certainly not be confined to a score or an IQ or achievement test. The test simplifies the recognition of some talents, but the complex potential of a child's talents, sustained interests, and special aptitudes cannot be represented by performance on a limited number of questions in a fixed period of time. We know our definition is more demanding, but it is much more accurate: Giftedness is the potential for creative accomplishment over a sustained period of time (years, perhaps even decades) in a number of different possible fields.

Let's look more closely at the three major parts of our definition.

The Potential for Creative Accomplishment. Giftedness is much more than getting good grades or high test scores. We're not opposed to good grades; all children should try to achieve their best in school. But in the real world of everyday life outside of and after school, giftedness is not usually measured by a good report card.

Someone described as a gifted architect would be praised for the way space, color, and texture are used in building designs, not for grades in Mechanical Drawing or Design Studio 101. A gifted architect's work shows beauty, originality, and imagination. Frank Lloyd Wright is regarded as gifted, not because of technical brilliance (which Wright's buildings frequently and notoriously lack), but because of his ability to recognize and express the harmony between a building and its environment.

How much a person knows or how quickly he or she has acquired that knowledge does not indicate creativity. A person's potential to use knowledge, information, or ideas in creative ways cannot be easily measured on a test because a new combination is involved. Giftedness is what a person can do with knowledge, how it can be turned into an original accomplishment.

Over a Sustained Period of Time. Definitions that rely primarily on test scores treat giftedness as a static concept. Either a child is gifted, or the child has "normal" or other levels of intelligence; the test results tell all, more or less for all time. Retesting may occur at various times, for test confirmation, but giftedness is seen as a fixed trait, as much a part of a child as eye color. If a child doesn't have it at test time, the child never will.

We believe that giftedness should be understood as the success achieved from one's efforts over many years. Creative productivity and genuine accomplishment can only be seen in a pattern over a long period of time. A person develops giftedness; it is not a "thing" one possesses. The proof of a person's giftedness should be that person's long-term accomplishments—the track record of all the races, not the first headline-making sprint.

In a Number of Different Fields. Test scores tell us about only a limited number of areas of human performance. By some estimates, a typical IQ test measures only 10 or 15 percent of the many abilities that have been identified and can be described with some degree of accuracy. IQ tests are a good measure of short-term memory, vocabulary, and spatial reasoning. But the tests miss creative imagination, leadership, social sensibility, interpersonal ability, artistic or musical ability, mechanical aptitude, and practical abilities ("street smarts"). Understanding giftedness in terms of an IQ score means over-looking or disregarding a number of talents that most of us would think of as gifts.

Achievement tests—Scholastic Aptitude tests (SATs) or statewide Regents' exams, for example—are little better than IQ tests as measures of giftedness. They claim to measure achievements rather than abilities, but achievement tests actu-ally measure the extent to which a person has mastered the specific material built into the test. If a school selects a stand-ardized test that covers the same material as the school's cur-riculum, then the test can give a good indication of how much the school's students have learned by test time. What students have already learned in predefined subject areas may be unre-lated to their strengths or talents outside of those areas.

To rely on achievement test scores to determine giftedness is to say, in effect, that people are gifted because they are good at giving the "right" answers in the areas the examiners decided are important. Students whose answers are valid but unortho-dox will very often not receive credit, especially on group tests or class quizzes. They don't have a chance to explain or defend their "wrong" answers. Reliance on achievement tests makes it easy to standardize the kinds of talents that are valued. What-ever their original intent, the tests seem to say: if we can't measure it, it doesn't matter. When standardized tests measure only a small range of the array of human talents, relying on them for a definition of giftedness may mean ignoring a num-ber of truly gifted people.

Implications of Our Definition

What difference does it make when you use our more contem-porary, broader definition of giftedness? One clue appears in the wording of this chapter's title. Traditional definitions lead to the question: How gifted is your child? They emphasize the child's *level of ability*—how far above average his or her test scores are. In some school programs, the need to pigeonhole students according to their scores has been carried to ridiculous extremes. For instance, IQ scores of 130–139 are "gifted," 140–149 are "highly gifted," 150–159 are "extremely gifted," and 160+ are "severely [?] and profoundly gifted." We have seen school officials and parents agonizing over whether a particular child was a genius, gifted, or above average but highly motivated—as if it made a difference to the child. Debates of this caliber are the educational equivalent of "How many angels can dance on the head of a pin?"

Our definition leads to a different question: How is your child gifted? This question challenges us to examine the child without searching for prevalued strengths, talents, needs, and interests—to identify the child's abilities and consider the ways in which they can be best encouraged. Our question is concerned with finding and building potential rather than battling about categories. Emphasis is moved from the test scores to the children themselves.

For us, "gifted" is an adjective that describes a child's accomplishments, not a label for the child. When we talk of gifted children, we are not referring to only a tiny group of people at the far end of the normal curve, a few rare individuals who are strangely different from the rest of the population. The potential for creative accomplishment—for behavior we would regard as gifted—resides in all children. Our challenge is to help parents transform that potential into reality.

We know that every child cannot grow up to be an Einstein, an Edison, or a Mozart. Not everyone is gifted at that level, but anyone *might be*. That distinction is important. Any number of factors come into play during a lifetime to determine whether a person will actually become creatively productive. The important goal with children is to find and encourage the right factors.

Many of these factors are external; they are not in the bundle of psychological characteristics that make up an individual. External factors may include the tools and techniques children are given the opportunity to learn to use, the support children get from family and friends, the environment or climate in which living, learning, and working take place, and the value our culture places on certain skills. A number of other variables can affect a person's fulfillment of potential: family role models, choices of spouse and friends, available learning opportunities, guidance and support of mentors, and, in all honesty, a certain amount of old-fashioned good luck.

No one can accurately predict how these factors will combine and contribute to the course of a person's lifetime. Some children will realize their gifts at an early age—our definition of giftedness leaves room for child prodigies. Others may never become productive despite all the best efforts to guide and nurture them. But we believe that the potential for creative accomplishment exists in everyone, and that the task of those who raise, guide, or teach children is to increase the degree to which anyone—as many anyones as possible—can make the best of his or her talents and strengths.

By emphasizing the potential present in all children, our approach includes those at the opposite end of the curve, away from giftedness. The current emphasis in educational circles is on keeping these "at risk" children from a life of complete failure. Their academic performance is poor and they are in danger of receiving failing grades and perhaps becoming school dropouts. The most these children are expected to attain is a life of mediocrity, a life in which nothing terrible happens but nothing too exciting occurs either.

We believe it is considerably more effective, both in the short and long range, to help all students—"at risk" or not—to learn how best to help themselves become successful learners. Not only do all children have the potential for creative accomplishment, but all children should have goals that will challenge them and a vision that will lead them to be the best they can be.

Is this view naive or idealistic, especially when we consider teens who don't know how to read or write? Can an eighth grader who can't read even a comic book be expected to become a Nobel laureate or win the Pulitzer prize? Edison was thrown out of public school and described as mentally addled and unteachable. Einstein had difficulties in school, especially with math. Anyone who has attended a class reunion may have found that the students voted most likely to succeed haven't amounted to much, whereas the class's "duds" or "dweebs" have blossomed. *We should be cautious about predicting a limited future for any child.* Instead, we should always leave room for youngsters to work toward challenges that are beyond "just getting by."

Don't ask "Is my child gifted or talented?" or "How gifted is my child?" Ask "How is my child gifted?" and "How can I encourage the best in my child?" As a parent, you can do many things to help spot your child's interests and talents and to encourage your child in reaching his or her fullest potential. Our goal is to help you discover and encourage that level of potential—to help you offer your children exciting new opportunities to be the best learners, the most creative producers, and the most gifted individuals they can be.

2

Finding Your Child's Unique Strengths

How can you recognize your child's potential? By seeking your child's strengths, unique characteristics, and sustained personal interests. This chapter provides you with strategies for discovering your child's abilities, creativity, motivations, and special interests. These strategies will help you to identify the way in which your child concentrates, processes information, and applies what is learned. Our purpose here is to provide you with the foundation for your efforts to bring out the best in your child. You will be building on this foundation throughout the book.

Recognizing Your Child's Best Characteristics

Modern researchers have identified several main sets of characteristics that enable people to become creatively productive (or gifted) in their behavior: ability, creativity, and motivation.

These characteristics are behind most significant accomplishments in almost every field of human endeavor—science, humanities, fine arts, and so forth. These characteristics can be as important in stimulating the best potential of children and adolescents as they are in describing the mature giftedness of adults.

These characteristics are **not** inborn traits that are either present or absent in an individual throughout his or her life. Instead, it is more appropriate to think of them as features that are akin to muscles—capable of being developed and exhibiting expression. The giftedness in each person represents the combination and development of ability, creativity, and motivation at a certain time and under the right circumstances.

Let's examine each of these characteristics separately.

Ability

A young child's understanding, memory, vocabulary, information store, reasoning, grasp of new information, recognition of relationships and connections among various ideas, and capacity for drawing conclusions and making inferences—all of these are the child's ability. Many people rely on tests to determine a child's natural aptitude for these mental processes, but there is valid evidence to support the conclusion that many—perhaps all—of children's ability can be improved through deliberate and appropriate instruction.

We believe it is important to recognize that these characteristics, which traditional views of giftedness have often treated as the total picture, are only the sky over the landscape. History abounds with people whose success would never have been guessed at by anyone who considered only their conventional abilities. Another important possibility is that test results might show a great deal of ability in a child's particular field of interest, without necessarily showing that same level of ability in other fields. Be concerned with *various* ways in which your child might express strengths; don't rely only on IQ tests.

Finally, don't let the word "giftedness" throw you. Giftedness is not limited to the one-in-a-million genius who has a statistically rare IQ score. Research shows that competent people of significant accomplishment do not necessarily have high IQs. Ability is relevant, but it is certainly not the *only* consideration, nor is it more important than any of the other characteristics we will discuss in this chapter.

Figure 2.1 describes the characteristics that are commonly held to be signs of intellectual ability and provides some

Figure 2.1   Evidence of Ability

Characteristics	Examples of a Child's Behavior
Displays advanced vocabulary for age group.	At age 3, Rana said: "Tony's birthday cake was elaborately decorated with prancing ponies and ferocious lions!"
Has good memory and large fund of information.	Ryan, age 6, recalls the names and characteristics of the dinosaurs he saw at the museum last year.
Learns new things quickly and easily.	Robert, age 9, was given instructions on the use of a computer only once and was able to run it on his own.
Generalizes and abstracts ideas adeptly.	Ricky, age 11, watched the evening news for a week and concluded on his own that, in a 30-minute program, only 11 minutes were devoted to news, whereas the rest of the time was given to weather, sports, or ads.
Comprehends new ideas in conversation and sees similarities, differences, and relationships.	Kerry, age 10, called the neighbor's new motorcycle an "Iron Horse."
Understands cause and effect, draws conclusions, and makes decisions.	Keith, age 9, understands the difference in the amount of heat absorbed by dark- and light-colored objects, and concludes that light colors should be worn in the summer.

examples of behavior that might be evidence of these characteristics in your child. (The items in the charts in this chapter
have been drawn from checklists originally developed by professional educators.)

Creativity

Creativity is the capacity to generate new ideas, to imagine
new possibilities and combinations, to look at problems from a
new point of view, and to take the risk of trying something that
has never been done before. Closely associated with knowledge, basic skills, and critical thinking, creativity could be understood as the use of knowledge and information in new
ways. Creativity is the foundation for all problem-solving and
decision-making skills.

Figure 2.2 shows some of the characteristics commonly associated with creativity and some examples of children's behavior that reflect these characteristics.

Motivation

Self-motivation, also known as *intrinsic* motivation, is a desire to
act that arises from within a person rather than as a response to
external incentives (systems of rewards and punishments, for
instance). Parents won't be surprised to hear that children often
do better work on a project that is closely allied to their interests
than on something far afield that they are being made to do.
The degree of self-motivation of a child (or an adult) has a strong
effect on the concentration given to working on a task, seeing it
through to completion, and striving for the best possible result.

Figure 2.3 shows some of the characteristics that reflect
motivation and gives examples of children's behavior for each
characteristic.

Figure 2.2   Evidence of Creativity

Characteristics	Examples of a Child's Behavior
Uses materials in unexpected ways.	Kevin has made candle holders, cooking utensils, and cooking grills from old cans.
Thinks of many ideas in everyday situations.	Don thought of a dozen different ways his brother might design a tree house.
Seems inclined to be a risk taker.	It was Judy's idea to become the first girl to play on the town's Little League baseball team.
Thinks independently.	Barbara questions the accuracy of the information in her history textbook's coverage of a topic, and desires to write to the authors about it.
Shows sensitivity to paradoxes.	Angela felt that it was funny for a commercial for diet soda to be shown in the middle of a cooking program about a rich, gourmet dessert.
Demonstrates flexibility, seeing things from different or varied perspectives.	Phil can cleverly use tools to accomplish many different tasks in addition to their usual uses.
Shows originality and can combine or transform ideas and objects.	Ken created a car for a soapbox derby entirely from spare parts and odds and ends from the garage and the basement.

Figure 2.3   Evidence of Motivation

Characteristics	Examples of a Child's Behavior
Becomes intensely involved in interests of own choosing.	Caroline frequently stays up late to finish reading a book, using a flashlight to read in bed after her bedtime.
Self-starts and does not need to be "pushed" to complete meaningful tasks.	After seeing a film about a UFO, Gene wrote and staged a neighborhood play about friendly space visitors; the play included sets, sound effects, costumes, and lighting.
Perseveres, not giving up easily on an important goal.	Although Mac had made several unsuccessful attempts to motorize a robot he was building, he continued on the project until he succeeded.
Has a high energy level, is eager to find new projects and challenges.	After spending two months on a science project, Tom was also eager to enter the Photography Club contest.
Likes to share ideas, products, collections, and so forth, and to invest time, energy, and resources in activities.	Phil has an extensive comic book collection and spends much of his time and money adding to the collection and swapping ideas and books with other collectors.
Assumes responsibility for important tasks.	When Mae was on a team for an art project, she worked many hours to build a structure before the deadline date. She persisted and encouraged others not to give up.

The Importance
of Sustained Interests

In addition to watching for ability, creativity, and motivation, you should be aware of your child's sustained interests—those that remain important over the course of months or years and don't fade a few days or weeks after the field trip, or visit, or other special event that first stimulated the interest. Encourage the short-term interests, but if reading a book or two from the library or doing a project on the topic seems to satisfy your child, don't push for any more involvement. Children can be curious about everything and anything. With a vast world of new things to catch their fancy, it is not unusual for their interests to shift frequently. Leave room for them to do so.

You may have to search for sustained interests for a considerable period of time. Children who have learned to be "adult-pleasers" often hide their best talents and interests when at home and at school.

When trying to discover your child's sustained interests, keep in mind these few tactics:

- Look daily. You never can tell when your child will discover something that will become a lifelong interest. Every day presents countless new opportunities and experiences.

- Discuss your child's interests at school conferences, to learn more about what the teachers have observed and to explore resources that are available to help students build on their special interests.

- Create opportunities for your child to pursue special interests outside of school. Design a den or a shop area in the garage or basement; help with finding materials;

search for places to go, projects to do, or other people or groups interested in the same topics.

Some Indicators of Sustained Interests

Your child will want to keep working on some things after the initial excitement has worn away. What does your child keep talking about? What activities reappear again and again? Those are the sustained interests you'll be watching for.

You can use the indicators in the following list to recognize your child's sustained interests. Bear in mind that the list is not designed to be a rating scale and that you cannot expect to see all of the indicators in your child. Instead, learn to use *any* of the following as an initial indicator—a sign that something is important to your youngster. A subject may form a sustained interest for your child if he or she:

- Completes assignments in the subject quickly and easily, with satisfactory (not necessarily *perfect*) accuracy.

- Reads widely about the subject, even in sources that are advanced or technical.

- Asks many questions about the subject that reflect prior study or complex understanding.

- Seems to have a "one-track" mind—eats, sleeps, breathes, walks, and talks the topic (sometimes to the distraction of others, including you).

- Brings projects to school to share with classmates or teachers.

- Involves the subject in other assignments (writes about it in English classes or paints it in art class, for instance) whenever possible.

- Keeps a log or diary of relevant activities and experiences.

- Talks about hobbies or career hopes that are related to the subject.

The Importance of Learning Style

During the past 25 years, research conducted at St. John's University (New York) and elsewhere has shown how it is possible to teach students either by implementing their individual learning styles or by teaching them to teach themselves by capitalizing on their personal style strengths. This research on learning styles explains why some children perform well in school and others (often from the same family) do not. There can be differences in style among siblings, between parents and their children, and among members of the same community, same occupation, and same culture. The research also explains how boys' and girls' styles differ and why some children learn to read early and well and others do not.

Everybody has a learning style and every style offers particular strengths, but each person's strengths are unique. Your style probably differs from that of your spouse and from those of each of your children. This is important to remember because parents frequently try to teach their children to learn in the same way that *they* learned when they were young. The result is likely to be frustration and failure for both parents and children.

What Is Learning Style?

Will a person learn best in bright light or dim? In a quiet room or with music playing? At a conventional desk or on a sofa (or in an easy chair, or on the floor)? Research shows that, to a greater extent than we would have thought possible, learning style depends on a person's biological makeup but encompasses more than biology. Emotional, sociological, physiological, and psychological characteristics—everything that controls how we concentrate on, process, and remember new and difficult information—contribute to learning style. We don't need to use our learning style when information is easy to understand, but we cannot learn difficult information easily without it.

For children to learn new and difficult information, they need to be able to concentrate on it, absorb it, and retain it—in a word, they must *process* the information. How does your child process information? Most children learn in one of two different processing styles—analytic or global.

Analytic learners ("analytics") learn most easily when information is introduced to them step-by-step or fact-by-fact. Analytics do not mind concentrating on what seem to be unrelated facts as long as they feel they are moving toward a gradual understanding. For example, you might teach an analytic how to read the word cat by explaining that the word has three letters: c, a, and t. The c in this word is called a hard c and sounds like a "k." The a is short and is pronounced as in "had." The t sounds like the letter "t" without the "-ee" part. Put together, the three sounds make cat.

Global learners ("globals") would find the analytic approach incredibly boring. Instead, globals learn best through short stories. When globals hear a story, they pay attention, particularly if the story is about something they recognize or something that interests them. Globals also learn through humor, illustrations, symbols, and graphics. They understand things better when they are introduced to them through an anecdote that explains what they need to learn and why they need to learn it. Once globals understand what they need to learn and *why*, they can concentrate on the details.

If you were teaching the word cat to your global child, you could start by describing how you felt something furry against your neck while you were asleep. You might explain how you were afraid. You opened one eye and looked around to see what was on your bed. You might laugh and say: "There was my *c a t,* and do you know what my *c a t* was doing? It was purring. What do you think my *c a t* is?"

Figure 2.4 contrasts preferences of analytics and globals. Both groups reason things out and are capable of mastering the same information or skills, provided they are allowed to use their particular strategy. Processing style seems to change as children grow older. Most elementary school children are global. The older they grow and the longer they remain in school, the more analytic some children become.

What is fascinating is that analytic and global youngsters seem to need different surroundings in order to learn well. Many analytics prefer learning in quiet, well-lit, formal settings. They often have a strong need to complete the tasks

Figure 2.4   Preferences of Analytics and Globals

Strongly Analytic People	Strongly Global People
Quiet while learning.	Sound (music, chatter) while learning.
Bright lighting while learning.	Soft lighting while learning.
Formal seating (hard chair, desk) while learning.	Informal seating (easy chair, lounge, bed, carpeting) while learning.
Working on a single task until it has been completed and *then* beginning the next task.	Working on several tasks simultaneously with "breaks" in between.
Snacking (eating, drinking, chewing, smoking) after they have completed their tasks.	Snacking (eating, drinking, chewing, smoking) *while* they do their tasks.

they are doing, and they rarely eat, drink, chew, or bite on objects *while* concentrating. Globals appear to thrive on distraction. They concentrate well against a background of music or conversations, with soft lighting and informal seating. Globals take frequent breaks and often prefer to work on several tasks at a time. They begin one task, stay with it for a while, switch to something else, and eventually return to the original assignment—and they repeat this pattern again and again.

Globals often prefer learning with other children rather than alone or under the direction of an adult. They like to structure tasks in their own way rather than follow someone else's direction. Most underachievers are global, but so are most children of very high intelligence. The difference seems to depend on differences in motivation and perceptual preferences.

What Is Your Child's Learning Style?

How well your child learns depends on how well your teaching style matches his or her processing style. Which style does your child feel most comfortable with, analytic or global? If your child has three or more of the following characteristics, you probably have an analytic:

- Concentrates best in quiet surroundings.

- Prefers brightly lit areas.

- Uses a formal desk, table, or chair.

- Doesn't snack or nibble while working.

- Follows a task through to completion or continues to a good stopping point.

Conversely, you have a global if your child:

- Concentrates best with music or background conversation.

- Prefers a softly lit area.

- Spreads out on informal furniture such as an easy chair or a couch, or on the floor.

- Snacks or nibbles or sips constantly.

- Studies with other children who have similar interests or talents.

- Takes short breaks and engages in a variety of activities at the same time.

It is important to remember that neither of these processing styles is better than the other. They are simply different and they should be approached differently. Perhaps 30 percent of all children are neither strongly analytic nor strongly global but may have characteristics that reflect both styles. With these youngsters, strategies from either style can be used; if they're interested in what they're learning, these children can absorb and retain in either style. However, the material you want them to learn must be made *interesting and relevant (to them)*.

How Can You Best Hold Your Child's Attention?

When addressing analytics:

- If the child is sound-oriented, speak directly to the point and say exactly what you mean.

- Itemize; list; summarize.

- If the child is sight-oriented, write the words or numbers that accompany what you are saying.

- If the child's orientation is tactual, touch the child's shoulder, arm, or wrist as you speak.

- If the child is kinesthetic, walk or rock or ride a swing with the child as you speak.

- Once you have explained what you want done (or learned), stop; do not repeat yourself.

- Begin with the facts and guide the child to an understanding of the entire concept.

When addressing globals:

- Explain your point through a story, anecdote, or joke.

- If the child is sight-oriented, illustrate your concept through symbols or caricatures.

- Use color to accompany drawings and stories.

- Begin with the overall idea; after it has been understood, focus on the details.

- If your youngster is peer-oriented, allow working with another child.

- Provide snacks.

- Permit breaks as requested and give short periods of relaxation between the heavy concentration periods.

What Are Your Child's Environmental Characteristics?

If you have two or more children, you may notice that one needs comparative quiet while concentrating on difficult materials and the other apparently works best surrounded by music, conversation, or noise. This difference creates problems in many families; one child is constantly humming and the other is just as constantly shushing. One studies with palms over ears because the other interrupts to talk things over every few minutes. One locks the door to keep intruders out; the other wants the television set on during all homework sessions.

Without an understanding of different learning styles, parents cannot appreciate that both environments—quiet or background noise—are normal and appropriate for different styles. Researchers have shown that when children are permitted to learn in ways that complement their unique learning styles, they achieve higher test scores.

If a child prefers to concentrate with music playing, parents should permit only music that has no lyrics. Even children who need background noise can be distracted by lyrics. Don't give in to "But they're not singing the words." A rendition may not include the words, but if the child is familiar with the song, the lyrics will get first attention anyway. As long as parents maintain the rule of no lyrics, children should be able to choose the type of music that makes them feel most comfortable.

Does Your Child Prefer Learning in Bright or in Dim Light?

When you were growing up, your parents probably warned you that if you read in the dark you would ruin your eyes. You may believe that a particular light level is necessary for good concentration. To the contrary, people's needs for bright or dim light vary. Some children need a great deal of light to concentrate. With less light, they become drowsy and literally cannot think. Others become nervous and distracted in what would seem to many to be perfectly normal illumination; these children concentrate better in a more subdued lighting arrangement.

The effect light can have on people is easy to demonstrate. What adult has not felt young and energetic on a bright sunny day and become listless and depressed when the weather was gray? But some people feel calmer and more assured in dismal weather; the brightness of sunshine *over*energizes them. You must determine the amount and type of lighting that your child needs in order to study well—and don't be surprised if different children need different levels of brightness. The amount and kind of lighting in the learning environment can actually increase or decrease your child's achievement test scores.

After you've determined how much light each child needs, take steps to provide it. If children share a bedroom, one side can be brightly lit and the other, softly lit. Experiment with different heights and placements of lighting fixtures and various types of bulbs. Look for lamps that accommodate three-way bulbs, and let your child choose the brightness setting. If your older children cover lamps with fire-proof scarves or banners, let them. That is their way of adjusting the light to be comfortable for them. If they aren't comfortable, they can't concentrate well.

How Does Your Child Respond to Temperature Variations?

Not everyone feels warm or cold at the same temperature. In any gathering of several adults, some will want the thermostat to be lowered or the windows opened wider, and others will insist that the room is too cold or they feel a draft. Certain people find it difficult to concentrate when they're too warm; others have the same problem when they're cold.

Individual physiological differences cause varied reactions to temperature. Still, most of us remind family, friends, and colleagues to dress warmer or cooler depending on how *we* feel, and we select or recommend the weight of our children's clothing on the same basis. Children who are either overdressed or underdressed are too uncomfortable to be able to concentrate on much else. Sometimes, the best thing to do is to let the children dress themselves. Given a little practice and some awareness of weather forecasts, most children will learn to judge how much clothing they need in order to be comfortable. At what age should you start letting your child choose what to wear? Perhaps at two or three? How early would you like to begin to develop the ability to make intelligent decisions? How early would you like your child to begin becoming gifted?

What Is the Best Seating Arrangement for Your Child?

You may equate the learning posture with sitting in a straight-back chair at a desk in a classroom, with feet resting firmly on the floor, back erect, and eyes forward toward the teacher. We do not know when or where it began, but this concept of the learning posture is far from necessary.

Ergonomics—the science of how efficiently people work with machines in various physical environments—has proven that people who sit for any length of time in seats without good back support find it hard to concentrate. Our own research shows that *some* people enjoy sitting on a wooden, steel, or plastic chair—the typical classroom furniture—and can work that way for long periods of time. Generally, these people become high achievers in school. But children who don't like that kind of formal environment can't concentrate and so can't remember what they have just been taught.

In our research, we allowed students who could not sit still for more than ten or twelve minutes in conventional school furniture to do their work in easy chairs, on couches, on bean-bag seats, or on the floor. These "informal" youngsters then did as well as the more formal ones. When we provided furniture that matched and mismatched each student's seating preference on an alternate daily basis for an entire school semester, we found the same results. Formal-preference and informal-preference students all did equally well when they were allowed to sit in furniture that matched their design preferences. Similar research has been conducted in South Africa with the same results.

During the past two decades, many schools have experimented with providing both formal and informal seating in classrooms, to let youngsters decide for themselves which design helps them learn best. In every group, the students' preferences tended to cluster: global learners seemed to think better with background sound than in quiet, to choose soft rather than bright light, and to concentrate better in an informal than a formal seating. Analytics preferred the environment the globals rejected. The two groups are equally intelligent and perform equally well, but only when their environment complements their learning style. Don't insist that your children study in an environment with which *you* feel comfortable. Instead, either let them work as *they* wish, or alternate their environments and observe the *results* of both conditions—their way and yours.

Responding to Your Child's Environmental Characteristics

As your child approaches the age of four or five, begin to consider his or her ideas concerning comfort and decor when planning the bedroom, playroom, kitchen, or living room spaces that the child will use. Don't buy furniture for those spaces without taking the child along. Seriously consider the preferences for quiet (versus noise), illumination, temperature, and seating arrangements that you have observed. Your child will be using some areas much more than you will, and if those special spaces in the home environment aren't comfortable, don't expect concentration or cooperation on important matters. It is hard to behave well when you're feeling uncomfortable. Give as much attention to your child's feeling at ease as you do to your own.

Before making any decision on design or furniture, seriously consider your child's learning style. Ask yourself whether your child prefers:

- Solitude and quiet, or being in the midst of activities, music, and conversation?

- Soft or bright lighting?

- Cool or warm temperatures?

- Bright or subdued colors for paint or wallpaper, fabrics, or accessories?

- Comfortable, informal, lounge furniture, or a more conventional, elegant style?

Answers to these questions will tell you, to a great extent, what sort of room would be best for your child—the ideal number, type, size, and placement of lighting fixtures; the most compatible decor; and the atmosphere most conducive to helping your child's strengths develop. Nurturing giftedness requires an atmosphere that permits creativity and talent to flow naturally.

What Are Your Child's Emotional Characteristics?

Is Your Child Motivated toward Learning?

Most young children are motivated to learn and experiment. When children recognize that something "comes easy" to them, they often enjoy the hard work it takes to further develop their ability into a talent. Few people have "gifts" in the sense that their ability requires little practice. A concert pianist doesn't make a career by sight-reading music. Rather, giftedness usually is the result of extreme dedication to improving an ability to the point where it becomes better than the same ability in competitors. This dedication often dies out among not-very-gifted children because their parents demand that the children be exceptional—good at something isn't good enough. Ask yourself whether you want your child to be gifted in order to enjoy a fuller life, or so that you have a showpiece. When parents *demand* that a child develop an ability, the child may feel that the ability is more important to the parents than he or she is as a person. The child may refuse to have anything more to do with that particular talent.

Children become and remain motivated when *they* enjoy what they're doing. When they feel good about their improvement, they begin to develop the sustained interest we discussed earlier. The decision as to which interests become sustained is one the child must make, *not* the parent. Expose your youngster to many different experiences and encourage pursuit of those that are of most interest, but leave the final choice up to the child, who will have to contribute the work and dedication needed to develop the talent.

Some children are so parent-motivated that, just to please the parent, they will devote themselves entirely to developing talents they don't really care about. When this is the *child's* choice, it is fine; many talented children became that way because they followed parental role-modeling or encouragement. But in cases of success, the child must *decide* to follow the parent. The choice must still rest with the child.

Is Your Child Focused?

Some children seem to be born for the tasks they get involved in. They have a long attention span for the things they are interested in and they finish what they begin. Teachers have long rewarded this sort of behavior and admonished less persistent children. As our understanding of the nature of persistence grows, we are finding that it is evident in some children from an early age and it never shows up at all in others. Analytic students seem to be very focused; once they begin a task, they move along step-by-step toward completion.

Global students, however, are not focused. They often learn in a completely opposite way. Globals consider a whole concept, idea, assignment, or endeavor. They need to plan the entire involvement in their mind, often for a long time, before they even *begin*. When they do begin, they generally work for a while and take a break, work again, and take another break. Because they often find it boring to stay with the same task without change, they may engage in a variety of activities at the same time. Global learners eventually complete tasks, but in their own interrupted way.

If you have a global child, you need to remember this pattern. Stop fussing over too many things being done at a time, and don't nag about getting started. Globals can't work that way. They need to think an entire project through before engaging in step one. Outsiders (and you *are* an outsider to your child) can't direct them. Their movement has to be internal. They have to *want* to engage in and complete the task.

If your child does not seem very focused, you have several choices:

- Divorce yourself from the situation and watch what happens; tomorrow is another day.

- Offer to help or share in the activity.

- Admit to yourself that this is not an activity that your child cares about.

- Drop the activity and replace it with something else.

Above all, do not criticize or embarrass your child. Other activities *will* be of interest, and a damaged self-image is far more serious than an incomplete assignment. Try to remember the times when *you* didn't want to complete a project or to do what you were told. Developing self-discipline is important, but it must be *self*-discipline if it is to be of any value.

Is Your Child Responsible?

Most adults believe that children should do what they are told. Generally, the adults are right. Following instructions is a requirement for growing up safe and secure. But when adults constantly restrict and structure a child's life, that child will never learn to self-start or make decisions. Conversely, an over-restricted child may become an extreme nonconformist who finds it insufferable to follow someone else's directions.

Authoritarian adults often rationalize their overly tight control with these arguments:

- If they were less strict, their child could get hurt.

- Their child needs tight control to be able to learn the skills necessary for functioning socially and professionally as an adult.

- Their child will never learn the difference between right and wrong without being made to toe the line.

These arguments have merit at times, but it is important to remember that a little independence is good for a child's safety (especially in resisting peer pressure), eventual success in a career (creativity doesn't come from following instructions all through life), and moral development (children learn right and wrong best through experience, and excessive control can shelter them from this experience).

Simple obedience in a child does not make a responsible child. Be aware of your child's need for opportunities to flex some muscles and find a different way. Allow opportunities for decision making in areas that seem important to your child, even when they change faster than the calendar. Require some conformity, but only when it is vital to you or to your child's well-being.

Is Your Child "Internally" or "Externally" Structured?

When children ask for explicit instructions about almost everything they do, psychologists refer to that behavior as "external structure." These children feel secure when they know what to do and how to do it. Others are more self-structured: they enjoy experimenting with a number of strategies and, eventually, doing what they do in their *own* way. Both of these types are equally capable, but, because of their different approach, they need different types of instruction.

If your child is always asking questions and seeking direction, provide it. Don't insist on thinking something through before the child is capable of that process or ready for the independence it implies. Provide a structure as long as one is needed. On the other hand, don't continue to be overly directive when your child wants to do things in a different way. Unless you have a very good reason for imposing your way—such as safety, or violation of public codes—allow freedom to experiment. Be directive about the issues that are at the *core* of your family, but not about every activity or viewpoint. In other words, choose your targets.

Responding to Your Child's Emotional Characteristics

To sum up the four emotional elements of learning style—motivation, focus, responsibility/conformity, and structure—

gifted children strive invariably for either things they enjoy or things they have a special talent for. They tend to be persistent in those areas, often providing their own structure. They *may* be conforming, but gifted children generally resist doing what they are told, perhaps because they see tasks differently. They often become excited by possibilities no one else has seen. They find different, better, more interesting ways to do everyday things, and they become increasingly inventive as their experience increases.

These "intuitive" characteristics may be the true joy of giftedness—the ability to soar beyond the ordinary. When doors are opened for such youngsters and they are permitted to find their own way on the other side of the sills, many children who have been carefully nurtured by their families enter into a world of their own. Their insights increase their motivation. Their task commitment fortifies their persistence. Their nonconformity rejects acceptable ideas that do not make sense to them. Their ability to structure their own pathways leads to independence.

Can you accept the possibility that your child's giftedness may lead into uncharted territories, sometimes leaving you behind? Answer that question to yourself before you read on. When you recognize that children concentrate differently and (when nurtured and supported) become capable of reaching different levels of creativity and intellectuality, you are ready to determine how much giftedness you are willing to liberate in your exceptional son or daughter.

Even if your children don't show the characteristics we've just described, try to accept and value and enjoy them as they are. No style is better or worse than any other. Be aware of what makes your children unique, and, as much as you can, respond to their emotional needs. Without catering to their every whim, allow these very special young people to be themselves.

What Are the Social Characteristics of Your Child's Learning Style?

Do You Have a Learning-Alone Child?

Parents entertain a number of ideas about child rearing, some more sensible than others. One of the less sensible ideas is that children should rarely be allowed to be alone and should have frequent access to others of their age. This simply is not true. Children should certainly have the opportunity to be with others, but they shouldn't be required to if they don't want to.

Often, the brightest children are self-motivated and enjoy spending hours by themselves doing whatever activities they find interesting. Toys, books, games, music, art work, sculpting, or their own imagination are enough to keep them in mental and spiritual health. For two children to play together is fine if they both want to, but parents who arrange such meetings to accommodate their own schedules or to try to force a friendship are doing their children a disservice.

Do You Have a Pair-Oriented Child?

Certain children play and learn best with just one other child present; others cannot cope with more than one playmate. Provide opportunities for individual, paired, and small-group interactions and see what happens. If problems arise, be sure that, in the near future, the number of acquaintances invited to be present at one time is restricted to your child's comfort level. After a while, you can try again to enlarge the number and re-evaluate the results. You should also pay attention to the type of youngster your preschool child prefers.

Do You Have a Group-Oriented Child?

Some children function best in a small group—the number that forms a team or attends a birthday party; many more children do not do well in groups. Allow each youngster to find a comfort level, and remember that the level varies immensely among children. Should children learn to get along with everyone? No; they only need to learn how to handle a broad variety of situations. Again, opportunities for socializing are one thing; mandates are quite another. Respect your children's individuality and, in time, they will respect both yours and their own.

Do You Have a Peer-Oriented Child?

There are children who only enjoy playing or working with people who have similar interests, talents, or abilities—and those people do not have to be other children. For instance, when an artistic, peer-oriented child meets someone with a similar talent, he or she may hover around the artist for long periods of time, absorbed in talking about, observing, and emulating everything the artist does. For such children, this kind of contact is an excellent way of expanding their interests and talents while helping them to understand the work and lessons and hours of practice an artist faces. To artistic children, the stimulation of knowing an accomplished artist may create the momentum needed to pursue their artistic goals.

Peer orientation becomes apparent among children who share interests in stamp collecting, building, music, singing, dancing, sports activities, and so forth. They begin to live and breathe for others who feel as they do. This is a positive reaction and should be encouraged—if the child chooses the involvement.

Does Your Child Need an Authoritative or Collegial Adult?

Some children respond best to an authoritative adult—someone who directs and provides specific guidelines. Other children respond best to a collegial adult—a person who acts like a friend rather than a parent, directs minimally and provides choices, and works with the child on a personal basis. Both types of adult are fine, as long as the style suits the child. Children who need a collegial parent feel alienated from an authority figure, and children who require authoritative grown-ups feel insecure with chummy ones.

Too many parents assume the role in which *they* feel most comfortable, not the one their children need. If they have two or more children, each one may need them to be a different type of person. Parents who are aware of their children's sociological needs can be both collegial *and* authoritative, playing the roles of teammate and umpire at the same time.

Does Your Child Learn in Patterns or Routines?

Some children feel most comfortable with patterns and routines; others love variety and tend to be adventuresome.

One child may want to do the same things over and over; another invariably tries new approaches and finds the unusual item the most interesting. These qualities often reveal themselves early in childhood; one child may beg to hear the same story again and the other asks for a new one.

As with other characteristics, neither variety nor routine is good or bad in and of itself. Children merely differ from each other. All parents have to do is become *aware* of their children's inclinations and respond to them.

Responding to Your Child's Social Characteristics

Avoid any predetermined beliefs concerning child rearing. The only generalizations that normally apply are that all children need to be loved, cared for, protected from harm, and accepted for their personal and learning-style traits. Giftedness can be developed among most children, but usually only in an atmosphere in which the child feels secure and respected. We have emphasized that each child is different from every other child. If you have more than one, be flexible in how you arrange their lives. Experiment with allowing your children to engage in activities alone, in pairs, with a small group, and with different types of adults until you sense that your child is comfortable. Unless safety is involved, let a choice of a group or pair stand. Because there is no "right" answer, almost any sociological pattern that matches your youngster's style will produce increased academic achievement.

What Are the Perceptual Characteristics of Your Child's Learning Style?

Does Your Child Learn by Hearing, Seeing, Handling, or Experiencing?

Grown-ups appear to be unaware that listening is the most difficult way for young children (and many adults) to absorb complex or comprehensive information. Yet we tend to teach our children by explaining things to them. With some it works: "auditory" learners can remember about three-fourths of what they hear. Unfortunately, less than 30 percent of the school-age population is auditory. Thus, when young children do not do the things they have been *told* to do, it is often because they find it difficult to absorb and remember them—particularly if a series of commands has been given.

Girls tend to be more auditory than boys. A female infant in a nursery begins to recognize familiar voices long before most male infants do. Young girls begin to talk earlier and more distinctly than young boys. When parents and teachers begin to teach reading by emphasizing what alphabetical letters sound like, most girls are better at it than most boys because they are able to hear and remember the sounds more easily.

This difference seems to continue throughout life. Grown women tend to be more verbal than grown men. Men tend to lose their hearing years before women do. Women appear to have stronger auditory memory than men do, and men tend to be visually stronger than women. Women often remember best the things they *hear,* whereas men tend to remember best the things they *see.*

At the most, only 40 percent of the school-age population learns visually—they are able to remember more than three-fourths of what they read or see. As a further complication, visual analytics tend to remember words and numbers and visual globals tend to remember pictures, illustrations, graphs, and symbols.

If preschool and elementary school children don't remember a great deal of what they hear or see, what *do* they remember? They remember what they touch, handle, and manipulate. We call such learners *tactual.* Tactual learners comprise our largest group of children. Another large group is kinesthetic children—those who need to *experience* what they learn. Such young people learn most effectively when they *do* something—take a trip, bake a cake, or build a birdhouse, for example.

Does Your Child Learn by Combining Several Perceptual Characteristics?

Some children have several perceptual strengths—exceptional talent in some or all of their auditory, visual, tactual, and kinesthetic capabilities. These children are most often considered academically gifted. Children who have only one perceptual strength can also achieve well in school as long as new material is introduced to them through that single perceptual channel. Children who have no particularly strong perceptual abilities must be taught through a multisensory approach that *begins* with their single best perceptual channel and is reinforced through other modalities. Most research shows that schoolchildren—gifted or not—will learn best when they are introduced to new information through their strongest perceptual channel.

Perceptual strengths develop at different rates in different children. Some start to learn difficult tasks through experience—what psychologists call kinesthesia. Next to emerge is usually the tactual sense; touching people and things excites the children's imagination and promotes memory. At age seven or eight, the visual sense kicks into gear, and about three years later the auditory sense emerges. This timetable has notable exceptions. Most schoolchildren remain kinesthetic throughout the elementary school years. Many high school students show no exceptional auditory aptitude, and some are neither auditory nor visual.

Responding to Your Child's Perceptual Strengths

Your child's perceptual strengths are innate gifts. You can't train them any more than you can train your child's height. All you can do is manipulate your child's education to complement the perceptual strengths and let learning occur as much as possible with as little conflict as possible.

Find out how your child learns. Is he or she primarily analytic? Global? Auditory, visual, tactual, or kinesthetic? Remember, a child needs only one perceptual strength to learn most things easily and well. Two strengths form a gift, and, for a child with three or four, the possibilities are almost unlimited. Because perceptual strengths increase and expand with age, your child may eventually develop more than one. In the meantime, find out which sense is strongest and use it to introduce all new material. For various combinations of your child's strengths, here are some activities and methods you can use:

- *Auditory and analytic:* Discuss whatever needs to be learned in small, sequential steps that build to an understanding.

- *Auditory and global:* Introduce what needs to be learned by way of an anecdote or two (explaining the concept or idea).

- *Visual and analytic:* Write words and numbers to reinforce what needs to be learned. (Be certain the child *sees* and *reads* what you write.)

- *Visual and global:* Illustrate what needs to be learned with pictures, symbols, shapes, and colors; the child should *see* what you draw.

- *Tactual and analytic:* Introduce difficult material through tactual resources (these are described in Chapter 5).

- *Tactual and global:* Introduce difficult material through tactual resources that can be approached through a story, anecdote, or game.

- *Kinesthetic:* Get the child into motion (walking, rocking, or pedaling a stationary bicycle); at the same time, give the child what needs to be learned, using his or her next strongest perceptual style.

In all these approaches, reinforce the new information through your child's next strongest perceptual strength, and then *apply* the new information through some original means, preferably something thought of by your child.

What Are Your Child's Other Physiological Characteristics?

Does Your Child Need to Eat While Learning?

The younger the child, the greater the compulsion to snack, chew, sip, or bite while concentrating. Mental challenges are accompanied by a craving for some kind of intake, especially among preschool children and adolescents. A wise parent provides nutritious snacks—raw vegetables and fruit, for instance—during brainstorming sessions.

What Is Your Child's Best Time of Day?

Research has shown repeatedly that learning is correlated to schoolchildren's body-temperature cycles; at all ages, they concentrate better at certain times of day. Even toddlers make known their bedtime preferences, and hyperactive children are usually most troublesome at regular times of day. According to researchers, only 28 percent of all schoolchildren are alert early in the morning; high energy between 6:00 A.M. and 9:00 A.M. is an adult pattern. Only a third of junior high schoolers are alert in the early morning. Prime learning time is about the same for all students: 10:00 A.M. to 2:00 P.M. As for "night owls," only 13 percent of all teenagers qualify, according to test data. Most kids are late morning or afternoon performers—far more conventional than they think.

Learn when your child has high energy and use those hours for exposure to important new concepts and skills. Reserve demanding tasks, such as homework or practice, for this best time of day as well. Check your child's schedule at school and try to get the best daily learning time assigned to the most important subjects.

How Much Mobility Does Your Child Need?

Most "hyperactive" children are not *clinically* hyperactive; they are normal youngsters in need of more mobility. The less interested they are in what they are learning, the more mobility they need. Anyone who has watched a boy squirming during a lengthy religious service can verify that statement.

Remarkably, nearly all children who need great mobility (95 percent) are *boys*. Girls who need a lot of mobility are often classified as "energetic" or "action-oriented"; boys are usually chastised in classrooms for exactly the same behavior. This dichotomy of response—and the fact that active behavior in boys is encouraged in the outside world and discouraged in school—can lead to serious role conflicts for young boys.

Studies have supported a distinction between true hyperactivity and some children's normal need for mobility. When previously restless schoolboys are reassigned to less passive, more participative and action-styled classrooms, their behavior is rarely even noticed. Some students thrive in activity-oriented environments; others prefer to remain in one place even when coaxed to move.

Almost 50 percent of all secondary school students require informal seating plans in order to concentrate, and a substantial percentage of healthy children have energy levels high enough to require constant mobility. To satisfy these needs, many schoolchildren—especially boys—sit in contorted postures, swing a limb, tap a foot, squirm, and even fall off their chairs. Your son's school should recognize his normal need for mobility and offer a variety of activities that will capitalize on his mobility strengths.

Responding to Your Child's Mobility

Most parents' learning styles are different from their children's. Parents who are outdoorsy and action-oriented may have children who are bookish and inclined toward less physical indoor games. Couch-potato parents may produce normally or clinically hyperactive children. Remember, children can't avoid being the way they are, whatever that way may be.

If your child appears to require activity most of the time, the burden of involvement falls on you, the parent. Because you are more adaptable than your child, you should try to get involved in the activity to which your child gives energy output, whether it is athletic, artistic, musical, or intellectual. If full involvement is beyond you, compromise. Express support of the interest, go to the site of your child's enthusiasm, get to know parents of like-minded children, and speak to coaches and mentors. Try to work in concert (rather than conflict) with the needs of your child. To develop your child's giftedness, you have to get involved knowledgeably in his or her interests.

As soon as you can, find out where your child's interests lie. Initiate *experiences* within those fields of interest. Giftedness develops from interest, blossoms into talent, and becomes skillful by way of practice. For practice to become a commitment, children must be challenged and encouraged by their parents or mentors.

Children who need a lot of mobility also need room. For some forms of play and creativity and practice, the child's usual play-space or even an extra (rumpus) room at home may not be enough. Find a park, a playground, a day-care center, a gym, or a library that offers the needed space or resources. If you can stand it, try to share your child's *physical* output—by jogging, working out, or playing catch. If you can't endure physical exertion, a formal activity program or another youngster's parent might be able to fill in for you.

If you are active and your child is more comfortable staying put, don't force athletic or mobile participation. Adapt, compromise, and acknowledge the difference between your preferences, but still try to become involved in what your child wants to do by expanding *your* sphere of experience to include it. As the parent, you are responsible for exposing your child to activities that will nurture giftedness.

Summing Up: Giftedness and Learning Styles

Giftedness should be considered to be a set of qualities or potentials that can be recognized and developed in children, not a mere label assigned to a lucky few. It awaits discovery in the abilities, interests, creativity, and personal motivation of children, and it can be nurtured by those who are willing to recognize and respect individual differences. To help make the best use of children's special abilities, parents and teachers need to be aware of children's processing styles, perceptual strengths, environmental preferences, and emotional and physiological characteristics.

Taking all these resources into account, you can build a richer, more complete profile of potential for your child. Some parents can determine intuitively, or by careful observation, the important elements of their children's learning style; others will find a more objective method useful. Our Learning Style Questionnaire (Chapter 7), based on extensive research into individual learning styles, will help you to determine the optimal learning situation for your child.

By recognizing and nurturing your child's strengths and abilities, you are well on your way to understanding and developing your child's unique giftedness. Because every child's learning style is unique, every child's giftedness emerges in a different way.

The Preschool Years

The time to start applying the advice given in the previous chapters—to start searching for and developing giftedness—is long before you send your child to school. For, although your child will probably get most of his or her education in schools, success in those schools depends in a large measure on the educational foundation you lay down during the first five years.

Preparing for a Baby

If you're a prospective parent, whether this will be your first child or one of several, the time to start developing your child's gifts is before its birth. Adhere to good daily health habits for yourself. Start eating a proper diet, at regularly scheduled meals, and add a good vitamin supplement to your prenatal menus. Give up smoking, alcoholic drinking, and any drugs not specifically prescribed by an obstetrician. Stay as far away as possible from fatty foods and polluted air and water. These suggestions may seem obvious, but they're too important to omit a reminder. If you'd like more information, your doctor can recommend the nutrition and exercise you'll need and tell you what you should avoid.

The Baby's First Three Months

Nurture your child's gifts and talents from the beginning of its life. The first weeks are full of opportunities to encourage your baby to discover the world through its senses. Although it is too early to start on such aspects of your child's giftedness as motivation, persistence, and learning structure, these other aspects will be built on the foundation begun during infancy.

Speaking to and Handling a Newborn

Whenever you are with your baby, speak softly, use a lot of repeated phrases, and try to make eye contact. Hold your baby during feedings and whenever else you can; hug and pat it gently. The need to be loved and accepted is particularly strong in growing children, and gentle contact is one of the best communicators of love and acceptance. Some researchers now recommend a great deal of skin contact between mother and child during the first twenty-four hours after birth.

There is no foolproof guideline as to how much attention each child should receive each day. Individuals vary considerably in the type, timing, duration, and variety of contacts they need, and common sense should prevail. Keep in mind too that the birth process is physically exhausting for the infant and that a newborn may sleep for long stretches during the first few weeks after birth. The baby's sleep should be interrupted as little as possible. Nevertheless, talking to and handling your child during waking hours will encourage alertness and readiness for skill development.

During the first few weeks of your child's life, avoid loud noises, jolts to the crib or bassinet, sudden shifts in position, and extremely bright lights. All of these can cause irritability among infants. Remind visitors to keep their voices soft and pleasant and to hold your baby securely, always providing head support.

Even young babies tend to imitate those around them, so *smile.* Let the infant begin to associate warmth and physical comfort with pleasant, positive facial expressions. As soon as the youngster can mimic, you'll get a smile back. This is the first stage in the learning process, your first opportunity to stimulate your child's giftedness.

Physical Reactions: Grasping and Holding

Somewhere between the first and third month after birth, children begin to stare at their hands. Eventually, they will reach out and grasp things, and perhaps hold them for a while. At this stage, baby-safe objects can be placed into their hands. The objects will be dropped often; pick them up and offer them again. As time goes by, encourage your child to reach out for objects that have a variety of sizes, shapes, and textures, for this is the first step in the evolution of curiosity and exploration.

Mental Reactions: Watching and Listening

A good way to encourage your baby's visual interest is to place two mobiles above the crib, one a foot or so to the right and the other the same distance to the left. (It's best not to put one directly overhead.) Mobiles that show colorful, familiar faces are probably better than most commercially produced concoctions, which appeal more to adults than to children. If you can find an inexpensive mobile, of any description, attach slightly larger than life-size pictures or drawings of familiar faces—mother's, father's, siblings', or grandparents'—to each dangling figure. Color the drawings with bright colors. Alternately, these faces could be strung from wire coathangers (with all sharp points or edges well wrapped in tape) using clip-on clothespins. The mobiles should be low enough to see but not so low that they are within the child's reach.

When your child is three or four months old, you might want to bolt to the side of the crib a steel arm from which you can hang a few large, brightly colored toys. Choose toys that have a wide variety of shapes and textures—three different toys, made of rubber, plastic, and wood, for instance. You want your child to grasp and handle these, so be sure that they're hung from the arm securely and that they have no parts that will break or fall into the crib. If your baby ignores the toys at first, don't worry about it. Leave them there and eventually curiosity and interest will take over.

When your baby becomes able to sit in an infant seat, be certain to move the seat around every so often, to introduce different rooms or areas of the house. Mirrors are appealing to youngsters as they become increasingly alert. Any mirrors within handling distance must be small, baby-safe, and unbreakable. Playing soft music during some of the child's waking time is another way to stimulate interest, particularly because the sense of hearing is more acute in babies than is the sense of sight. Talk and read to your youngster, and listen carefully. Be ready to encourage any attempts to imitate or respond.

The Foundations for Learning: Three Months to Two Years

Based on his extensive studies of the intellectual and emotional development of very young children, Burton White recommends a series of toys to be introduced to children at different stages of their development. White urges parents not to give in to advertising pressure and buy expensive, commercially produced toys. Manufacturers, he says, often are unaware of the ages at which their toys are most appropriate for children. Instead, White suggests that parents should build their own toys, using baby-safe paints and materials.

Bear in mind, as we describe these various toys, that different children will respond to them in different ways. A child who takes an interest in a given toy before most children in the same age group is ahead of his or her peers *in some ways*. A child who tends to respond to an item later than most is probably more sensitive in some other area. Some differences in response are so extreme that no one has been able to pin down a "normal" age at which a child is expected to do something. There is at best an average age *range,* and even that should be understood as an educated guess.

If your child is bored with or frustrated by a given toy, put it away and try it again a month later. If your child seems to be interested in a particular toy and it has no safety risks, try it now regardless of when it was "scheduled" for play. It matters more that your child is interested in a variety of toys than that a particular toy is played with at a certain time.

As you allow your child to play with these toys, you may have to learn to tolerate the mess and noise that can result. Try and contain the mess—restrict the finger paints to the bathtub or the basement, for instance—but don't skip an activity simply because it is not neat. A child in the heady throes of learning is rarely neat, especially where the learning involves water, paint, or sand.

Three to Five Months

One of the best beginning toys is a baby-safe stainless steel mirror placed over the crib, six or seven inches from the baby's eyes and positioned so that the image can be noticed. As children grow, eventually they will recognize their own face and realize that, as they change their expressions, so does the figure in the mirror. They will start to make faces at the figure and learn to manipulate their features in interesting ways. (If you have a video camera, keep it handy when this toy is in use.)

Locate or make an inexpensive crib gym that features a few simple items your baby can handle, strike, or pull. A kick-toy suspended close enough to be kicked without knocking it loose will provide exercise and entertainment. Another good source of exercise is a large, vinyl-covered surface attached to a strong elastic strip and strung between the crib uprights. It will bounce back as your baby kicks and pushes at it.

Finally, invest in a good, stable infant seat, to give your baby a change of scenery from time to time. Keep the seat near you while you work, entertain, or relax. You don't have to keep the child in your presence at all times, but the more stimulation your child receives, the more alert it will become. Again, remember that not all babies will respond to these toys at this age. If you set them up and your baby ignores them, don't worry. Leave them in place, and they'll be ready when needed.

Five to Eight Months

At around this age, your baby will probably begin to entertain itself by dropping and throwing down small objects. Try to bear in mind as you pick up these things over and over that this is a healthy sign of growth and an activity you should encourage. Instead of scolding your child for throwing things, provide a good supply of multicolored unbreakable objects (large enough so they can't be swallowed) to fling around. Part of the fun for the baby is seeing where things go when they are dropped. If you get tired of picking them up and have an older child, take turns with the older sibling in fetching the bombs-away items.

When your child begins to crawl, make some relatively open floor space safe for the child to move around in. Playpens are fine up to a point, especially when no one is free to keep an eye on the baby. But your child will need some time in a more open area to properly develop leg muscles and to prevent boredom.

Childproof a room for your child to explore. Arrange the furnishings so that there are no electrical or phone cords to pull, no heating elements or breakables within reach, no steps to tumble down, and no sharp edges to run into. Then turn your baby loose and let the exploration begin! Talk encouragingly, perhaps (if you have the patience) naming the objects that are touched or of interest. Not only will your baby find your voice soothing, but talking to infants, especially during a time of keen interest, helps develop their sensitivity to speech and sound. Children who are spoken to a great deal tend to be more expressive than those who are not.

When your child can move around a little, various sized balls that can be rolled around and retrieved make terrific toys. Again, choose a variety of different shapes, sizes, and textures of toys, and be certain none of them is small enough to swallow. Add a few plastic bowls and cups, and your child will spend hours putting balls into the containers and dumping them out again. In the process, important spatial and motor skills will be learned. You can keep the interest up by rotating the items from day to day; add new ones, then replace them with old familiar items from time to time.

At this age, your child may take an interest in stacking toys—plastic cups that nest, rings that can be dropped on a pole, and boxes of various shapes that fit inside each other. Plastic bowls, such as those used for margarine or whipped topping, and measuring cups will often prove as interesting as commercially available toys.

If you have the space, a stable, well-built walker can give your child another chance to explore. A walker also provides a better chance to get into trouble: it raises the child high enough to pull attractive (and sometimes dangerous) items off tables or shelves. If you let your child use a walker, *never* leave it unattended.

We have mentioned that restrictive devices such as playpens, cribs, jump seats, highchairs, and play-and-feed tables are valuable when you can't supervise your child constantly. But they stifle movement and, after a point, can limit intellectual development. True, a child who spends a lot of time in a restrictive device will eventually learn everything that would have been learned if freedom to roam were allowed more often. But the learning is postponed to a later stage of development. Realistically, you *have* to put your child into a restrictive device sometimes, but if you can, allow two or three hours a day to be spent exploring his or her world, unrestrictedly.

When you are reasonably sure your child can actually speak a word ("Mama" or "Dada" usually comes first), encourage talking as much as you can. Declare the speech attempts wonderful and say how proud you are. Above all, talk to your child about anything. What you say may not be understood, but your child will hear the approval in your voice and see it in your face. Realizing that you are pleased, your child will want to please you even more by acquiring new skills.

At about this age, some children show they can follow simple instructions, such as waving good-bye or giving you a toy you request. You should give your child ample opportunity to exercise these skills (wave good-bye every time you leave the room) and, as with speaking, give praise whenever they're demonstrated. Remember again that children need different amounts of time to learn this sort of behavior. Don't worry if your child doesn't learn right away, and give no less praise for the later learning.

Eight to Fourteen Months

Most children at this age are extremely curious and have an overpowering need to explore. White insists that this urge is the main motive behind children's acquisition of intelligence. Your best approach at this time is to give your child as wide a variety of experiences and as free a rein as your schedule and sanity will allow—bouncing, catching, dodging, galloping, kicking, rolling, running, skipping, swinging, and throwing. It is especially important to allow a girl to explore these various skills at this age. If she can learn how to enjoy these activities, she can better resist society's attempts to condition her into thinking she should be passive, unathletic, and "ladylike."

Continuing language development is critical in the growth of verbal intelligence and reasoning ability, as well as for social maturation. During this period, babies reveal that they not only respond to certain words but they have begun to understand their meaning. Children comprehend words before they say them but, by the age of two, most appear ready to verbalize their understandings. Your child will react to simple requests to pick up an object, wave good-bye, come toward you when you call—or run away if the "terrible two" stage has started! Speak to your youngster, show and name interesting and colorful items, describe things inside and outside your home, use adjectives while simultaneously pointing to the quality you are emphasizing, and reward cooperative responsiveness to your statements with hugs, laughs, comments, and pats. These efforts will be rewarded by the onset of speech. Indeed, you will be delighted and astonished by a rapidly increasing ability to communicate with you and others.

Girls are more likely than boys to express themselves early and skillfully. One of the differences between the sexes is that most females become able to remember what they hear at an earlier age than most males. Thus, girls will repeat, speak, and engage in conversations with a wider vocabulary long before boys—although, certainly, *some* boys develop early auditory skills. As a result, generally speaking, girls begin kindergarten with a wider vocabulary and begin to read earlier than most boys. Conversely, many more boys than girls have speech problems and experience difficulty when reading. Despite your natural concerns, do not be unnecessarily alarmed if your son's initial speech is less articulate than you had anticipated; his normal aging will improve his ability to express himself clearly.

Most children learn naturally as their experience and curiosity about others and themselves widen. During this stage, they begin to want to master certain physical activities. Youngsters of this age have what White terms "a full natural agenda." Imposed teaching may bore your youngster and have negative effects. Remain at ease with the child, be supportive, and provide language opportunities through everyday experiences and as opportunities present themselves. Many children enjoy pantomiming their communication efforts. They wave when they say "good-bye," throw a kiss and say "love you," pick up a utensil and say "want," and move appropriately while saying "dance," "walk," "jump," and other descriptions of their ongoing activities.

Balance is as central to speech development as it is to good child rearing. Love and nurturing must be balanced by sensitivity to lack of interest, boredom, or stress. If you don't insist that an achievement be learned or demonstrated today, your youngster may be ready to do so tomorrow; if you mandate attention or mastery today, your child may become nonconforming and refuse to do the activity for a long period of time. At this stage, focus on speech and other learning activities more than on obedience or safety measures. Successful parenting includes firmness as well as support. Give support and direction at this stage, without sliding into permissiveness.

Under your control and supervision, build your child's learning skills through exploration, exposure to new experiences, play, and the handling of a variety of items. Provide opportunities to "find" things by encouraging reaching for an item hidden behind another object. Show that some objects bounce and others do not. Encourage the placement of smaller objects inside larger containers. Suggest feeling different textures and listening for specific sounds. Developing sensory awareness contributes to the refinement of keen perceptions. In this critical stage for rapid learning growth, you can use your youngster's natural curiosity as a springboard to giftedness.

Fourteen to Twenty-Four Months

At about this age, children start to build their language and social skills. Their already considerable curiosity continues to increase, and they finish laying the foundations of their intelligence. Talk to your child a great deal, mentioning the names of familiar people and objects in short, simple sentences. Introduce music more prominently, through recordings of catchy children's songs, particularly the ones that involve miming, clapping, and stamping. Don't assume your child isn't interested in your talking—keep talking and let the child communicate whether what you're saying is of interest. When you see attention starting to wander, then stop.

Your child will often be willing and eager to talk to you at this time. Encourage dialogue. Answer questions as patiently and as completely as you know how. Ask the child to describe colors and shapes to you. Offer some simple choices of different actions and describe the advantages and disadvantages of each one.

You have probably been taking your child out for some time now, so you can start to go on "pretend" trips together. Re-enacting a trip to a restaurant or a store or grandma's house helps reinforce your child's vocabulary and imagination. After dramatizing an event once or twice, your child will be more aware of details on the next trip and will probably remember more of what happens. A toy telephone helps to build verbal and imaginative skills, as do dolls and adult figures. When you choose bedtime books about adult figures, include people in a variety of roles (farmers, police officers, chefs). Expand your child's imagination beyond mommy and daddy and the daily environment.

Balls of various sizes remain an appealing toy at this age, especially if a hardwood floor is available for bouncing. Pots, pans, and plastic bowls still hold their fascination as well. This is a good age for a four-wheeled wagon. Your child will enjoy being pulled around and will give rides to his possessions. Pulling a cart full of blocks gives your child a hands-on demonstration of gravity, friction, weight, and counterforce—but don't use those terms yet.

At this age, your child will probably become interested in playing in and with water. Allow extended, supervised play in the bathtub or in a wading pool, or, if the climate is right, with a lawn sprinkler. Common household items such as measuring cups and plastic bowls can provide as much fun as commercial toys. Make a game of guessing whether something will float or sink. Find a few absorbent mats for the bathroom floor, and try not to worry too much about the mess.

This might be a good time for a sandbox, if your child has learned not to eat sand or dirt. Either build or buy a simple, smooth-surfaced enclosure, a ten-pound bag of sand, and some different sized plastic pails and shovels. Most children start to find sandboxes fun at this stage and continue to play in them for many years, so plan on a sandbox that will last.

If you are handy with tools, you may want to build some of these toys yourself. A toy you build will probably last longer than a commercial product, and it certainly will be appreciated more by your child. Enlist a "helper" while making the toy, and let the child decorate it with paint and/or stickers. Both of you will have fun and you'll encourage your child to pick up similar skills. Other items you can make are child-sized furnishings (a small rocking chair or small cushions), a swing, a balance beam (about a foot wide would be best to start), or a small jungle gym.

If you haven't already begun, this is a good time to initiate what should be a lifelong habit—reading with your child. Research has found that the most capable youngsters come from homes filled with books. Choose short stories that have familiar figures in them, such as babies, toys, or grandparents. Point out simple words and ask your child to find them elsewhere on the page. Discuss the story a week or so later and see whether the child remembers the plot and characters. Give your child the gift of reading early and encourage it throughout his or her life. (It helps if you enjoy reading yourself.)

Toward the end of this stage, children begin to want books of their own. Choose simple books with easy-to-turn pages and large, colorful pictures. Cloth and plastic books are more durable than paper ones, but neither type is entirely childproof. Buy inexpensive books and try not to be upset at torn, folded, or drawn-on pages. Little children enjoy ripping, folding, crinkling, and twisting paper, and this is what many of your child's first books will be used for.

General Guidelines

The division of infancy into different age groups gives more of a range than a rule. Children develop at very different rates, and no child is going to develop all of these interests to the same degree. If your child never seems to care about pretend trips or doesn't start playing in water until mid-third year, don't worry about it. Encourage your child in areas of apparent interest, and don't try to force activities that get a negative reaction or indifference.

The Larger Tools of Learning: Ages Two to Five

Motivational Differences

The first two years of your baby's life are devoted, for the most part, to the exploration of the environment and the development of the skills needed for further exploration. Starting with the third year or so, the tasks your child learns become more specific and complex, such as doing a jigsaw puzzle or riding a tricycle (and eventually a bicycle).

At this time, you can start to understand how your child is motivated toward achievements. Some children are self-motivated; they require only time to teach themselves what they want to learn. Others are peer-oriented and won't try something unless they can get one or more friends to try it with them. Others are authority-oriented and need an older person to show them how to do things and watch them try. Once you understand what moves your child to try something new, you can start to adjust your teaching method to that learning style.

Ways to Stimulate Further Learning

We've already recommended finger paints for very young children. At about two years old, many children begin to enjoy crayons and clean, white pieces of paper. Learning to draw allows children to experiment with color and line and gives their imagination free rein. If you find your child has an interest in drawing, encourage it as much as you can. Talk about what the drawings show and praise the completed work.

Simultaneously, your child will probably start to build with building blocks. Earlier play with blocks may have consisted of dropping them from the crib or floating them in the tub. Now the child should be able to create things with them. Again, encourage the interest, show the different things that can be done with the blocks, and praise all successes.

Your child should be old enough now to start caring for toys. Show how to use each new toy responsibly. This is the time to start teaching that everything has a place where it belongs and should be returned there when playtime is over.

The role playing you started with your child at a younger age will expand now to adopting different roles and imagining visits differently from the way they happened. One way to encourage this sort of experimentation is to arrange visits to different places. Age two or three is, for most children, not too young for a first trip to a fire station, an amusement park, or a petting zoo. Keep in mind that your child still has a short attention span. Don't make the visit overly long.

This is the age when your child will actively start to watch television. Though virtually unavoidable, we don't encourage making television more than an occasional activity. Television does have some advantages; it can help your child develop verbal skills, and programs such as "Sesame Street" can introduce numbers and some simple mathematics. But television has three disadvantages that outweigh the advantages. First, it is habit-forming. Many children (and adults, for that matter) will turn it on and spin the dial just to see what's on, without an interest in any program in particular. Second, television is essentially passive. Children should *do* things, not just watch them. Finally, television is nonchallenging. It doesn't encourage children to think or reflect, the way most other activities do. Children need to make reflection a habitual part of their lives if they are to grow up to be truly fulfilled adults.

Owning a VCR can counteract some of network television's disadvantages. Selection is involved, a good antidote for "seeing what's on." Watching films together can create a good family activity while encouraging an ability to critique content, theme, and acting skill. Look for videos that support your child's activities and interests. Hobbies, trades, sports and physical conditioning, and travelogues are all available and can be a supplement or guide for personal efforts to learn or to improve a skill. A VCR can widen the scope of the television screen while it limits its use to constructive viewing.

If your child's television viewing is starting to dominate all leisure time, the best thing you can do is to turn the set off and substitute an alternate or outdoor activity.

Developing Independence

By the time your child reaches the age of two, your encouragement of the natural tendency to explore should have built up a degree of independence, and your praise of achievements should have led to a degree of self-confidence. Your child will begin to use these traits for building other skills.

At this point in your child's development, you should start to serve more as a resource than as a trainer. Introduce your child to a new task or toy and then withdraw, coming in to help only as needed. After age two and a half, your child will learn to recognize when assistance is needed, so be careful not to jump in and help until you are asked. When you do help, show what is needed and then let the child try again alone. Be available to help without taking over, because the more your child can do without assistance, the better new tasks will be learned.

There is a fine line between giving your child enough independence for self-teaching and so much independence that the result is frustration. The best way to walk that line is simply to watch your child carefully. If he or she seems intent on working things out alone, don't volunteer to help. If frustration starts to show, offer help. And if your help is refused, respect the refusal. Many of the more determined children get great satisfaction from working out difficult problems for themselves. Encourage this type of satisfaction as much as possible.

In addition to helping your child when needed, encourage your child to help you—and be certain the things you do together are not just the domestic chores. It's perfectly all right for your child to help you bake a cake or dust the furniture, but your helper should also be included in building and repairing items around the home, tending the house plants or yard, shopping, and joining you in your hobbies or sports. To some extent, your child may watch as you participate, but it's not too early to start to teach how to do the things you enjoy. A three-year-old won't handle a bat or racquet very well but will start to develop an interest in the games and some coordination. By age four, the child will be ready to start on the practice needed to become a good player.

It's a good idea to talk to your child in adult language (no profanity, please). Children who are exposed to an adult vocabulary all their lives will find it easier to learn to read. They will develop a more extensive vocabulary and a better aptitude for the language than children whose abilities were hampered by parents who used only nonsense words or baby talk during the child's formative years.

Finally, when children (or adults) realize they have done their absolute best at some task, they feel a sense of achievement that psychologists refer to as a peak experience. Besides being rewarding in themselves, these peak experiences help to develop the self-confidence and strong self-image that will lead to other peaks. When you give your child an opportunity to succeed at a difficult task, you will not only be teaching that task but preparing him or her to face future tasks with confidence. As the old proverb says, nothing succeeds like success.

Cooperation and Competition

To reach their highest potential, children have to learn both to cooperate with others and to compete against their own abilities. You can help encourage cooperation in your child by:

1. Setting a common goal.

   "Let's build a doghouse together."

   "Why don't we plan a party with three of your best friends."

2. Dividing up tasks and delegating responsibility.

   "You put the parts together as I read the instructions."

   "John, you and Bill decorate the table while we get the food ready."

3. Spreading the rewards among the group.

   "Grandma and grandpa can't believe we built the doghouse ourselves. They said it was a professional job."

   "You know, everyone loved our party."

When you teach your child to cooperate, you are helping to develop a recognition that a group needs contributions from all its individuals to work together well. Your child will learn to deal constructively with others, to work toward a common goal, and to take responsibility for assigned tasks. All of these skills will be beneficial in later life.

Working with a group also gives your child a chance to exercise creativity in solving a problem because it requires a child to:

- Contribute ideas;
- Paraphrase and clarify the ideas of others;
- Express support and acceptance of others;
- Encourage others to contribute ideas;
- Summarize and integrate the ideas into a plan;
- Coordinate the efforts of different group members;
- Give direction to the group as a whole.

When you set up group activities for your child, make sure the satisfaction for the group comes from completing the task, not from beating some other team at all costs. The best form of success is success in reaching a personal goal.

There is room for some healthy competition in your child's life. Most children will not get involved in a given field unless they feel they can succeed in it, and success is most easily measured in competition against others. Also, success in a competition helps to build children's self-image and confidence in their abilities.

Competition, in sports or in other activities, can be a healthful way to promote personal achievement. It can be sad to lose a race, but it is even sadder to never take the risks of entering. Children start to become aware of their abilities at around age three, and will look for approval of their achievements. Most often, this approval will be couched in the language of competition. It is important for you to recognize this development when it happens and respond to it.

For instance, if your child has learned to ride a tricycle and tells you proudly that the neighbor's child hasn't, you should recognize that this is a bid for approval and praise the achievement accordingly. Too many parents will say something like "You did learn to ride before she did, but I'm sure she can do other things better than you." Presumably, this sort of response is intended to keep a child's ego in check, to prevent development of a sense of superiority. But downgrading abilities can keep your child from developing the self-confidence that will be helpful later in life.

Your child's belief in an ability to succeed begins with *your* belief that the child will succeed. If you show your belief, your child will pick it up and will be able to approach new tasks without being undermined by fear. You began to build your child's belief in self when you encouraged exploring the environment and experimenting with various blocks and balls as a toddler. From these activities came learning how to make things happen without assistance and being confident enough to try other things. Now, by regularly trying more and more difficult tasks—and by having each success recognized and praised—your child will learn that he or she can do nearly anything. "I can do it" are beautiful words when spoken by a child.

In the best sense of the term, *competitive* people are interested in doing things well and in having their achievements compared favorably to those of others. When your child takes the risk of competing against others, it is a sign of confidence in the ability to achieve. Encourage participation in games that require a winner or two. Tell each winner that he or she played well. Tell each loser that no one can win all the time and encourage trying again soon.

Some children's games—dodgeball, catch, ring-toss, wiffle ball, or spud—not only build confidence but can also increase powers of observation, self-control, and the ability to solve problems. Be sure to encourage a wide variety of games involving many different skills, especially if you have more than one child in your family. Every child will not excel in the same areas, and you should allow each child to find and capitalize on individual strengths and earn an equal portion of praise. Like most people, your child will learn more from strengths than from weaknesses.

As children reach four years of age, they should be encouraged to participate with groups in things they can do well. If they are athletically inclined, arrange for your child's play group to play baseball (with plastic bats and balls), minibasketball, or miniature golf as part of a team. If they are artistic, invite the group over for a "painter's party," where they can all draw, paint, or sculpt, and then hold a small exhibit. If they enjoy music, encourage them to have a show in which each one gets a few minutes on stage to perform for a family audience or a gathering of parents. Whatever their skills may be, provide small group get-togethers that highlight various interests and allow comparison of their talents to the talents of others. They will not only learn to recognize where they excel but will have an opportunity to learn from watching others.

As your child's self-confidence builds, expect some self-protection—avoidance of areas in which he or she can't compete or that are not of interest. If your child doesn't want to compete in a given field, respect that wish. Remember that some children excel easily but don't enjoy competing against others. Let them be themselves and don't apply pressure.

The purposes of competition are to build self-confidence, develop skills, and teach the value of teamwork. The purpose is not to have a child win at all costs; that attitude is not the best way to produce winners. A winning team wins because it works well as a team, because there is cooperation among the team members, and because each member contributes to the whole. This is the true goal of competition and this, rather than the external rewards of winning, should be the source of your child's satisfaction.

Learning about the Arts

From the time your youngster is three or four years of age, initiate learning about the arts through trips to museums, concerts, and the theater. It's best to choose artistic events that interest *you* and then take your child along. But even if you're not thrilled with children's theater productions, attend them with your child occasionally to create an awareness that these events are available. Any outings can be fun as long as you remember that your child probably won't be interested for very long (perhaps only fifteen minutes or so at the beginning) and may not appreciate the experience until attending becomes a more familiar routine. As you continue exposure to various arts and express your own appreciation for them, an appreciation for the arts will slowly come.

When you take a child who is between three and five years old to the theater or to a concert, be prepared to see only the first part of the performance. Young people's shows, where fairy tales and children's classics are dramatized, are an excellent introduction to the theater, and outdoor concerts are often appealing to children, particularly if they include energetic dances.

A child who is exposed to the arts may want to take part in them. Indeed, your child may have a latent talent for painting, dancing, or playing an instrument that doesn't come to the surface until these arts are seen being performed by others. If your child shows an interest in an art form, encourage the interest as much as you can. *Don't* choose an art form and insist that your child become good at it. Your child should be allowed to choose how energies will be channeled, and the arts are only one alternative.

Anticipating Consequences

One of the skills that will best help your child grow is the ability to anticipate the consequences of actions. This trait may seem simple and obvious, but it is a specific talent that many people don't develop because they have never received any training directed toward developing it.

You probably give your child some training in anticipating consequences without realizing that you're doing it. When you see juice being poured too quickly into a small glass, you yell "Be careful or you'll spill it." When a portable radio is in use, you say "Turn it off when you're done with it or the battery will wear down"; when a toy is being wound up, you warn "Not too tightly or it will break." Most parents give these sorts of warnings automatically and don't need to be encouraged.

But warnings such as these are only one way to develop the skill of anticipating consequences. A far better way is to encourage children to figure out the consequences without being told. Many children have never had to learn to think about the outcome of their actions because they have received constant warnings from their parents.

The age at which you should begin developing this skill varies from child to child, but it is usually safe to begin between the ages of two and three—depending on your child's maturity and willingness to learn. You should increase awareness of consequences between the ages of three and five.

The way to encourage thinking about consequences is to describe a situation and ask what the outcome might be. You might even make a game of it, starting a short story and letting the child fill in the ending. As a simple example, you could ask:

"What would happen if we have paint on our hands and don't wash it off?"

"If we left the toys outside when we came into the house, what would happen to them?"

At a more advanced level, you might try:

"A lady was baking a cake. Her telephone rang, and she went to answer it. She talked on the phone a long time and forgot all about the cake in the oven. What do you think happened to the cake?"

Because each story can have more than one ending, your child has a chance to exercise some imagination. When you get one good answer, you may want to praise the answer and then ask for another. Be careful not to push too hard for consequences, and if the child doesn't seem to like this kind of coaxing, drop the subject and try it again a few months later. Eventually, you may want to encourage the child to make up cause-and-effect questions for you to answer, although most children will do this without being asked.

Using Imagination and Building Creativity

Storytelling and dramatizations are ways to develop your child's imagination and intellect. Read books aloud daily, as many as will be tolerated. After a story becomes familiar, ask your child to tell it to you, perhaps while looking at the pictures.

When your child is four or five, start asking questions that require changing places, imaginatively, with someone else: "What would you do if you were [a character in a story]?" This kind of role playing is a difficult skill, and you have to be sensitive as to whether your child is ready for it. If no idea of what he or she would do in a given situation emerges, suggest what you would do and then drop the subject for a while. Eventually, after hearing your ideas and being exposed to more stories, your child will begin to learn how to imagine actions in other situations.

There are four different aspects of thinking, and you should be aware of them and consciously use them when encouraging the development of your child's imagination:

1. *Fluency*—Give your child the opportunity to talk about *many* alternate possibilities.

2. *Flexibility*—Encourage your child to think of a wide range of possibilities and to see a situation from several different viewpoints.

3. *Originality*—Encourage your child to think of unusual, new ideas.

4. *Elaboration*—Discuss your child's ideas in detail. Ask questions that fill out an idea and make it more interesting.

Chapter 6 provides a series of practical activities that will help encourage your child to think creatively and critically.

Promoting Skillful Thinking and Problem Solving

One of the earliest thinking skills your child will learn is counting and comparing. It's very easy to overdo instruction in counting, and you should be careful not to insist on it too early. From about the time your child is two years old, whenever you see a picture of two of a kind, say something about the two figures, such as "Those two trees look very tall," or "I wouldn't like to live in either of those two houses." Eventually, your child will learn to recognize sets of two, three, and four. In a similar way, you can teach comparison of sizes, colors, shapes, and distances.

From the age of two on, introduce your child to simple problem solving. For instance, if you were to read a story about a little boy who went to visit his grandma and forgot his toothbrush, you could ask your child what the little boy probably did about brushing his teeth. If your child can't think of anything, ask "What would *you* have done if you had forgotten your toothbrush?" Chapter 6 suggests some specific activities for encouraging your child to solve problems.

Never push your child beyond where he or she is ready to go. Children mature at different rates, and each one is capable of considerable achievement in some area at some time. But most children require additional experience before they're ready to function well in a variety of skills. Be careful not to make your child feel inept or incapable in a given area. A skill that can't be performed yet may only need time.

We've mentioned role playing as a way to spur your child's imagination. Another skill to be gained from role playing is the ability to understand the motives of others. There are a number of good reasons why your child might find this sort of understanding useful:

- Reasoning ability is sharpened by helping to focus on people and the situations they find themselves in;

- Someone else's thoughts can be anticipated, which is helpful in competitive ventures now and for years to come;

- How someone else thinks or feels can be pictured, an exercise in imagination that can lead to such creative ventures as writing or acting.

The best way to teach empathy for others—in fact, the best way to teach most of these skills—is by demonstrating this ability yourself. For example, if someone has been curt to you in your child's presence, you might say "He probably isn't feeling well" or "He wasn't really thinking about how he would make me feel." By suggesting reasons for the behavior of others, you will start your child thinking along these lines.

In addition to role playing and teaching by example, you can suggest possible reasons behind some of the behavior children see. Try to be realistic and imaginative without being cynical. For instance, if someone on one of your child's teams asks another player to join in, some possible reasons might be:

The group is short one player.

The player who made the invitation may be a better player who wants to teach the less skilled player (or may want to see whether he or she is a better player than the invited player).

The player who made the invitation may be trying to be nice to a neighbor.

The invited player is a good player whom the team wants for the game.

The team simply likes the invited player.

Explain these various alternatives through questions, suggestions, storytelling, and analogies, and encourage your child to offer other possibilities. If your child isn't ready for this sort of mental gymnastics, let the matter drop for a couple of months and then try again. Often, the intellectual seeds you plant will sprout in bunches.

Formal Teaching at Home

In addition to all the informal techniques we've suggested throughout this chapter, many parents are now devoting their time and energy to a more formal preschool instruction at home. These formal efforts can often be helpful, but if you decide to try at-home instruction, you should remember that three things are essential to making the effort successful:

- *You should enjoy teaching* and the pleasure you feel should come across to your child. Your own enthusiasm will go a long way toward sparking an excitement for learning in your child.

- *You should be patient and supportive.* Children should not feel pressured to achieve or inadequate when they cannot. They may understand some things immediately and need an hour or more to comprehend others. Remember that children learn in different ways and under different conditions. If something you've tried hasn't worked, then you may have to adapt your methods to your child's learning style.

- *Your child must be willing to learn.* Don't coerce your child into working on something that he or she doesn't want to do. There is no quicker way to turn a child away from learning for life. Never bribe your child to learn. When he or she is ready, you'll be asked to "show me." Children are ready to learn when they start asking questions. They are willing to learn when you approach them with activities and they respond with interest. By the age of four, many children are ready and eager to learn to read— particularly when older siblings are already reading. Start whenever your child is willing and pause whenever you see signals that it's time to stop.

A Final Word:
Overcoming Self-Defeating Mechanisms

Over the past few years, researchers have identified a number of self-defeating emotional characteristics that keep individuals from fulfilling the potential of their lives. Some of these are:

- A need for approval that is so strong that they don't try things that others may frown upon;

- A concentration on past traditions, incidents, or situations that so restricts their progress that they conform completely to traditional role models or blame a lack of progress on a bad childhood experience or on other people;

- A degree of guilt or worry that keeps them from getting involved in different activities;

- A fear of the unknown that is strong enough to keep them from trying something unfamiliar;

- A frustration stemming from experience of a lack of justice ("They make it so hard for girls to succeed that fighting the system just isn't worthwhile.");

- An unconquerable procrastination.

Emotionally well, self-actualized people don't groan, complain, or accept setbacks. Instead, they cope with problems as they arise, and they make the best of their situation. They don't pretend they're happy when they're not and they don't have any need to impress others with their abilities. They enjoy whatever they make happen and then move on to the next experience. If they find that something needs to be changed, they work to change it and enjoy the whole process. They admit their mistakes and try to avoid them in the future.

Emotionally healthy people are energetic, idealistic, persistent, ambitious, intellectual, outgoing, highly individualistic, and loving toward others and toward themselves. They are extremely active yet enjoy solitude at times. They appreciate nature, interesting people, new places, and a wide variety of experiences.

The activities we've suggested for raising your child from birth are designed to help develop these characteristics. The best way to teach your child to value these characteristics is by valuing them yourself.

4

The School Years—Making Them as Valuable as Possible

Parents and Schools—Common Goals

Parents and educators share some very important goals for children. Both are concerned with promoting the growth and development that will contribute to students' success later in life. Both share a desire for children to learn to be successful problem solvers so that they can grow into resourceful and autonomous people. These shared purposes are too often overlooked by educators and parents, who sometimes seem to choose to interact as adversaries rather than partners.

Your own supportive attitude will help you and your child's teachers develop a partnership. In turn, the partnership will help your child to explore and develop his or her abilities as fully as possible. As you cooperate with the teachers at your child's school, keep in mind that, although the child they teach is the same person you send out the door each morning, neither of you sees that child's entire life. You know some things about your child that the people at school won't see, and there are other behaviors *they* will see but you will not. Neither of you will observe all of your child's behaviors; others will be noticed both at school and at home.

Parental Goals

It is important for you to understand the trends in attitude that influence school policies and teaching methods. Once you know these, you will be able to fill in the gaps in your child's fundamental knowledge and thinking skills, which may be addressed only superficially in the classroom.

During the 1960s, the schools trumpeted innovation and discovery methods, new math, and problem solving—sometimes ignoring basic facts and skills (such as memorizing multiplication tables). Since that time, the pendulum has swung back toward teaching basic facts and fundamental skills. Currently, the press criticizes the schools for the inability of schoolchildren to think cognitively and to solve problems—not to mention their failure to score well on basic information tests.

The central truth is obvious: children must have both basic skills *and* the ability to think through and solve problems. Parents can help because learning occurs both in and out of school and should be a lifelong process. What you do with your child at home can promote the ability to think, solve problems, and make decisions, assuming the schools and teachers take care of basic knowledge and skills.

In addition to developing thinking skills and informing with basic knowledge, educational goals for children should include developing a lifelong love of learning, a good self-image, gifts, talents, and creativity. Parents should try to work cooperately with schools to promote this cumulative philosophy, to make every schoolyear as valuable as possible for all children.

The following sections deal with various elements of teaching and the learning environment that are important to consider in developing your child's giftedness. Some parents will have more control over and input into their child's formal education than others will. *Ideally,* one would be able to choose a teacher best suited to a child's learning needs and to influence the teaching environment, teaching methods, and so on. In reality, this is rarely possible. Therefore, it is all the more important that educators are seen as partners in bringing out your child's unique gifts and talents and that you attempt to work together, in partnership, toward that end.

Teachers' Styles

Teachers receive standard professional training, but each teacher's approach, background, and abilities vary, just as do those of doctors, lawyers, dentists, and architects. Style has become part of the professional lexicon, the nonmedical equivalent of "bedside manner." A teacher's style is critical to the learning process. A close match between your child's learning style and the instructor's teaching style can all but guarantee a child who will be successful and happy in school.

Planning

A lesson plan should reflect a teacher's judgment regarding each student's ability, development stage, learning history, interests, and learning style. From the teacher's lesson plan come specific goals, advice and counseling, decisions on the child's physical placement in the classroom, and the sequence of assignments. Your child will benefit greatly from this type of personalized attention.

If at all possible, before your child is assigned to a specific teacher, ask whether the teacher:

- Diagnoses each student's ability level, interests, and learning style;

- Prepares lessons, projects, and assignments for small groups or individuals;

- Plans whole-class lessons only when appropriate or necessary;

- Provides creative activities with student options;

- Assigns peer tutors or uses other cooperative learning strategies;

- Gives some students the opportunity to design their own studies.

Methods

Teaching methods and techniques generally refer to the instructor's activity in the classroom—use of various resources, ways of working with students, and approaches to learning in general. Teaching methods may include lectures, questions, games, simulations, programmed learning sequences, computer programs, independent study, role playing, and cooperative learning. Ask whether your child's teacher:

- Lectures (if so, for how much of the time);

- Uses media and computers;

- Engages in class discussion;

- Demonstrates, dramatizes, or uses role playing;

- Divides the class into small groups;

- Distributes assignments and directions based on individual needs;

- Plans with individual students;
- Assigns independent study for certain individuals.

Environment

The teaching environment includes a room plan that reflects how the instructor divides, designs, and decorates various learning areas. Furniture arrangements, seating assignments, formal and informal spaces, offices, and workstations all comprise the teaching environment. Because the teaching environment affects how students are grouped (individually, or in pairs or teams), time schedules, varied learning activities and resources, and directions for student mobility and snacking, you should ask whether your child's teacher:

- Permits only traditional rows of desks;
- Provides individuals and small groups with alcoves, dens, offices, or learning centers;
- Designs both informal and formal workstations;
- Provides or at least permits nutritional snacks, drinks, or water as needed;
- Consults with students about where they may sit and do their best work;
- Provides a variety of multisensory resources;
- Arranges alternative learning activities for mobile, active students.

Evaluation Techniques

A teacher's evaluation of a student's progress should not be limited to test scores. Information on student growth should include observation of performance, self-evaluation, and a variety of testing approaches to confirm whether the child is gaining in knowledge and skills, reasoning ability, and creativity in other areas. Therefore, ask whether your child's teacher:

- Observes student progress by moving from group to group and among individuals;

- Designs tests that measure whether objectives are being met;

- Requires students to measure their own progress;

- Uses student performance as well as written tests to determine what students have learned;

- Considers alternative individual measures such as projects, audio and video tapes, inventions and designs, drawings, and diagrams in addition to standardized test scores.

Teaching Characteristics and Classroom Management

Teaching characteristics are defined as the values and standards a teacher holds and how they are imparted to the students. The instructor's flexibility, the learning elements stressed, and the type and amount of direction given are all part of classroom management. In this regard, the rules and procedures used to build the learning environment should leave room for the many different learning styles found among the students. Ask whether your child's teacher:

- Cares about how students learn best;

- Has different assignments for individuals and small groups;

- Maintains a high standard and demands the best from all students according to their ability;

- Evaluates students' progress as they learn;

- Believes in individual progress more than grade-level standards;

- Varies the group lesson plans to meet individual needs;

- Changes teaching styles to motivate individual students.

Educational Philosophy

All teachers have certain beliefs about education that influence their teaching styles. Often, they teach either the way they were taught when they were young or the way they are required to teach by their supervisors. These beliefs can become ingrained and can influence the teachers' decisions and attitudes. Parents should seek teachers whose beliefs match their children's learning style needs. Ask whether your child's teacher, principal, and school district believe in:

- Open-ended assignments and teaching strategies;

- Alternative educational programs;

- Grouping of different ages;

- Matching of teaching and learning styles;

- A student-centered curriculum;

- Behavioral or performance objectives;

- Independent study;

- Individual or personalized instruction;

- Self-directed student learning as well as direct instruction, as appropriate.

Figure 4.1   Determining Teachers' Preferences for Particular Student Types

Student Characteristic	Teacher's Preference			
Learning Rate	Quick achiever	_____	Slow achiever	_____
	Average achiever	_____	Nonachiever (apparently)	_____
Motivation	Self-starting	_____	Apathetic	_____
	Conforming	_____	Nonconforming	_____
	Persistent	_____	Not persistent	_____
	Responsible	_____	Not responsible	_____
Emotional Stability	Highly stable	_____	Emotionally troubled	_____
	Active or mobile	_____	Impulsive	_____
	Quiet and passive	_____	Reflective	_____
Learning Potential	High achiever	_____	Average in verbal skills	_____
	Creative with school tasks	_____	Below average in verbal skills	_____
	Above average in verbal skills	_____	Learning-impaired	_____
Gifts	Articulate	_____	Problem solver	_____
	Athletic	_____	Decision maker	_____
	Artistic	_____	Visionary	_____
	Inventive	_____	Mathematical	_____
Independence	Peer-oriented	_____	Independent	_____
	Adult-oriented	_____	Authority-oriented	_____

Preferences for Student Types

Teachers have preferences—conscious and unconscious—for certain types of students. As you consider the best match for your child, try to profile each teacher's preferences with respect to the characteristics in Figure 4.1 by placing the teacher's initials next to the preferred category. If you are not able to determine a preference in each group, mark with an X the preferences you think are most important for your child's progress. The right teacher or a teacher who does the right things may be critical to your child's school success.

Meetings with Your Child's Teacher

When the schoolyear is underway, your conferences with the teacher (or principal, if necessary) should be friendly and supportive. With most teachers, you will be able to communicate best in a mutually helpful atmosphere, so don't try to force teachers and administrators to become defensive. Make the following activities your goals in the meetings:

- Focus on your child's progress with respect to the school goals, but describe his or her strengths and learning style.

- Look for specific examples of results in class; probe beyond generalities such as "I enjoy having Billy in my class."

- Determine how—in which specific areas—you can help the educational process at home.

- Describe and give examples of the intelligence level your child exhibits away from school, whether in reading,

mathematics, the arts, athletics, or other accomplishments.

- Ask the teacher for an appraisal of your child's learning
  style strengths and how you both can meet his or her
  individual learning needs.

- Plan joint projects with the school to take advantage of
  your child's gifts and special intelligence.

- Work through any differences you and the teacher may
  have in how you perceive your child's progress and level
  of happiness.

Consider changing to a different instructor if your child
shows signs of:

- Continuing unhappiness

- Extreme apathy

- Depression

- Destructive tendencies

- Violence toward siblings

- Disorientation

- Crying bouts

- Nervousness

- Chronic physical symptoms (upset stomach, headache,
  and similar complaints).

There could be other reasons for these symptoms—family
crises, the death of a loved one, and many others—but if the
symptoms seem to be connected directly with school, look into
the trouble. There are literally thousands of teacher behaviors

that could lead to poor learning in some children. You'll be able to predict some poor matchups—a teacher who insists that students sit up straight in their chairs, when you know your child thinks best when sprawled on the couch; or a teacher who will not recognize inventive, alternative answers and insists there is only one "right" answer for each question.

Teachers, by and large, want to be successful. You can help them by discussing your child's learning style, intelligence, gifts, and other strengths. Review the section in Chapter 2 on identifying your child's learning style. The descriptions of teaching style in this chapter should help you to identify the right teacher for your child, help the teacher to understand the best ways to work with your child, and, if it should prove necessary, help you to explain to the principal why you feel a change is essential.

Programs for the Gifted Child

Since the mid-1970s, there has been an increasing emphasis in schools on creating special programs, or even special schools, for "gifted students." How do these "gifted programs" relate to your concern for bringing out the best in your child? The easiest way to answer this question is to tell you that there is both good news and bad news.

The good news is that the development of gifted programs has been a positive influence in public education. In part, these gifted programs have had the following desirable results.

1. *Increased awareness.* The gifted programs have alerted more teachers and administrators to the importance of stimulating their more capable students. In the past, many admonitions about "respecting individual differences" have come to focus on only how to reach students with learning difficulties or

on the special needs of pupils with physical handicaps or social and emotional problems. Gifted education has shown the importance of recognizing individual strengths and talents, thus stimulating educators to think about bringing out the best in all learners.

2. *Leadership for innovation and change.* Gifted education has often been a source of innovations in instructional programming. Many contemporary advances in instructional practice—in such areas as critical and creative thinking, problem solving, and independent study—have been brought into schools through gifted education specialists and programs.

3. *Continuing education opportunities for teachers.* Through gifted education, many classroom teachers have found new opportunities for advanced training in learning styles, thinking skills, small-group instructional strategies, and ways to adapt instruction to individual differences among students.

4. *Disappearance of myths about capable students.* A greater awareness of gifted education has helped break down the following common myths about bright students:

- Bright students don't need any help. They'll learn the material anyway.

- If students finish an assignment early, they should simply wait quietly for the rest of the class to finish.

- Enrichment means giving students twice as much of the same kind of work to do.

- Young children who read early or do things before others their age are smart alecks or they have been pushed too hard by their parents. The best thing to do for them is to teach them to fit in with the group.

- Everyone in a class should work the same way, on the same assignment.

- Gifted students get perfect papers on every test and assignment.

The bad news about gifted programs is that they have given rise to the following regrettable practices, among others, in many schools.

1. *Narrow conception of giftedness.* Gifted programs commonly focus only on traditional intellectual abilities (i.e., IQ), often dressed up in terms such as "academic gifts." This focus tends to define giftedness as a fixed, predetermined trait. Such a narrow view doesn't allow for the nature and development of human talents and abilities and is likely to limit the range of the school's efforts to develop the best among its students.

2. *Overemphasis on test scores and labels.* The casualties are diagnosis of the students' needs, and the search for the best way to help students learn and grow. Even when schools break out of the traditional paralysis of IQ scores and talk of using multiple identification criteria, those criteria often are other test scores that are highly correlated with IQ scores (such as scores on standardized achievement tests). More important, when only test scores and rating scales are used as selection criteria, the usefulness of these scores in planning instruction is lost completely.

3. *Excessive focus on the selection process.* Decision making in gifted education has all too often revolved around the number of students who can (or should) be admitted into the programs. Sometimes this emphasis arises from a misunderstanding of statistics; many educators (and budgeters) believe that if only the top 3 to 5 percent of the population is gifted, then programs should be limited to the top 3 to 5 percent of the student body. Because this understanding is based on the narrow view of giftedness as measured by test scores—IQ scores in particular—we don't hold the admission approach in very high regard.

Even if we were to agree that gifted people make up only the top few percent of the population, this premise doesn't mean that every sample taken from the general population (such as the student body of a single school or school district) would be limited to that exact percentage. In some schools, a third of the student body might be gifted, by our definition; other schools may hold only one or two gifted students. Programs for the gifted should not be mandated for a given percentage; they should be as large as they need to be.

A rigid quota system on gifted programs may stem from a school's rightful concerns about limited resources. When little can be offered, a school will want to make sure that its resources are not diluted by trying to provide too much for too many students. The argument usually favors limiting participation to those who are the most highly gifted. Unfortunately, when it comes down to defining them, the "most highly gifted" are usually those with the highest IQ-test scores, which again imposes the limited definition of giftedness.

Rather than treating a test score as an absolute entitlement for participation in the gifted program, why not consider the instructional needs of the student? We think it's crucial for all educators, and for those in gifted education in particular, to place less emphasis on selection, inclusion, and exclusion, and more emphasis on effective instructional planning and on services that are designed to help all students become as successful as possible.

4. *Single, fixed "gifted programs."* Too many schools have viewed gifted education as a matter of creating and conducting a single program of one kind or another, on the assumption that such a program will meet the needs of all gifted students. In many school districts, especially at the elementary school level, the program is most often a "pull out" program, in which students are taken out of their regular classrooms for a fixed period of time (often a half-day or full day each week) to attend

special classes in another room or at another school. At the secondary level, some resource room programs exist, but it is more common to offer special "tracks" or advanced classes for high-ability students.

Good educational programs can never be "one size fits all." No single program can respond to the broad range of strengths, talents, potentials, or sustained interests that are represented by our concept of giftedness. If the goal of effective programming is to bring out the best in any student, then a broad array of programs is called for—not just a single program to which any student is given either admission or exclusion on the basis of test scores. Any school should contain different kinds of programming that will stimulate its students, each according to his or her gifts.

Goals and Expectations for Quality Education

Both parents and educators recognize that people expect more from their schools than ever before. As the complexity of our world increases and our children face more difficult personal and social challenges than any previous generation, the demands on education increase. We realize that knowledge, talent, imagination, and good judgment are far too important to be wasted because of substandard education. As a society, we have an urgent need for well-educated specialists in a number of fields, in order to continue improving the quality of life (and perhaps to ensure our survival). Schools share in the responsibility for nurturing these specialists. Their giftedness will be needed to sustain basic elements of our society, including:

- Science, medicine, technology, and engineering—to find solutions to the problems of hunger, disease, and the destruction of our living environment;

- The social and behavioral sciences—to solve the problems of injustice, inequality, and prejudice through educated leadership and relevant studies;

- The arts, culture, and entertainment—to provide the creative expressions that add joy and meaning to life;

- Ethical, moral, and religious principles and philosophical analysis—to guide individuals and groups in how to deal effectively with the complex challenges of human existence;

- Personal fulfillment—to enable individuals to live in greater mental, emotional, and physical health and to celebrate their own talents as well as those of others.

No one can choose which young people have the greatest potential for accomplishments in these various fields because gifts in these fields often develop over the course of an individual's life. They are the products of many complex factors beyond the quality of education. Nevertheless, educators today are rightfully called upon to make their best possible effort to nurture students' special needs, interests, and potentials. Increasingly, our schools must serve as the guardians of the future. There are several steps you can take to contribute to their success:

- Promote systematic efforts in schools to seek out and help develop the potentials of both students and teachers.

- Support the schools' programs for valuing and rewarding excellence.

- Encourage your school to risk innovation in the recognition and development of talents.

- Stimulate your school's efforts to recognize individuality and to encourage independent, responsible self-direction.

- Support additional training for teachers and administrators to help them recognize and nurture students' talents.

- Endorse the effective use of community resources to expand learning opportunities for all students.

- Campaign for more awareness of the academic, personal, and emotional characteristics associated with giftedness, and support teachers' efforts to respond effectively to gifted students.

- Encourage ongoing efforts in schools to develop ambitious goals and promote their attainment.

From this list of goals, it's easy to infer some of the earmarks of a high-quality gifted program, which are shown in Figure 4.2. Look for these characteristics in the programming at your neighborhood school, but keep in mind that excellent programs are the result of *years* of careful planning and development. They don't come about quickly or by chance. Consider not only how your school is meeting some of these goals, but also its ongoing efforts to expand their fulfillment.

As you go through the list of characteristics of good gifted education, it should become clear that your responsibilities as a parent run considerably deeper than asking whether your child will be allowed to take part in the program. You need to ask a number of much more specific questions. It may be easier for the school to talk about cutoff scores or selection procedures than to discuss your more complex concerns. Approach the school with a constructive attitude and try to avoid frustrating and fruitless arguments about the right or wrong way to define gifted programming, but remain firm and aggressive about finding the best possible instruction for your child. Focus your conversation on your child's needs rather than on what's wrong with the school's programming.

Figure 4.2   Evaluating Gifted Programs

Characteristics of High-Quality Programming	What Parents Can Look For
Teachers and administrators show support for recognizing and developing the strengths of each student.	Written and oral communications from teachers and administrators describing your child's characteristics and needs.
School officials value input from parents and other community members.	Planning committees include parents and members of the community; frequent parent/teacher conferences and opportunities for parental participation.
School's definition of giftedness is up-to-date and inclusive.	Program literature cites recent theory and research, and an inclusive approach is evident in meetings with staff members.
Purposes and goals are clearly stated and emphasize commitment to meeting the needs of all students.	School has formulated a written statement of its program's definition, goals, and procedures.
Commitment to an identification of gifts that is flexible and inclusive; recognition of students' unique needs is stressed rather than arbitrary procedures emphasizing fixed percentages, cutoff scores, or funding issues.	In written material and conferences, evidence that the school seeks and responds to your child's characteristics, talents and interests, rather than to lists of tests for placement in a program.
Support for all teachers to search (individually and cooperatively) for the strengths, talents, and sustained interests of their students.	Evidence that children have the opportunity to take part in activities they are interested in and to be involved in planning and conducting projects of their own, either individually or as part of a group.

Figure 4.2   *(continued)*

Characteristics of High-Quality Programming	What Parents Can Look For
A good balance between the unique demands of each developmental level and the need for continuity during children's school career.	Provisions for passing information about children's gifts from one grade to the next. Trust your judgment about the quality of the response you get, and ask for specifics, not generalities.
Commitment to integrating all the components of the school's program; a program that includes many staff members and has options that support and enhance the regular program rather than compete with it.	A comfortable fit of activities that are part of the gifted program with the school's overall program and with how teachers ensure that all students are challenged. Again, look for specifics.
Programming that is concerned with the ways the students learn best and with their educational needs, rather than with rewarding "good" behavior.	Signs that the teachers may be using gifted programming as a reward; meaningful work, not just drill and repetition. The key question is: what work does your child *need* in order to learn?
Routines and procedures that can be modified (or ignored) when necessary, to ensure that gifted students' needs will be met.	Killer excuses, such as: "You can't take part in this program because you'll miss your spelling pretest" or "You can't take that section because the computer won't schedule it that way." (Humans should always be able to override the computer.)
Commitment to provide varied services—within and beyond the regular school program—to the diverse needs of the student body.	Evidence that the students are given more than a single "gifted room" that offers the same program for all gifted students; programming efforts that

(continued)

Figure 4.2 *(continued)*

Characteristics of High-Quality Programming	What Parents Can Look For
	include: learning style assessment; both independent and small-group projects; access to various learning resources; services for many different talents and areas of interest.
School documents its activities carefully for all students, reports regularly on students' work and accomplishments, and involves parents in their child's education.	An active role in your child's activities, beyond just signing a permission slip; information on the programs and activities your child is involved with, preferably evidence of a learning-style diagnosis; regular conferences to discuss your child's progress; a good program that keeps communication with the parent open throughout the schoolyear.

How You Can Support
Your School's Efforts

We have been talking about what you can expect from a high-quality school. You should be working in partnership with your school to make or keep it high-quality, and a partnership requires contributions from both sides. To develop the best in your child, you and the school will need to work together. Too many people are ready to decry what's wrong with today's schools and how much education has deteriorated since their own school days. Find out about the *good* things that are happening in your school, express your appreciation, and let other people in the community know about them.

Any school is certain to have room for improvement. Don't head for your easy chair after you tell the teachers, the administrators, or the School Board what's wrong and what *they* can do. Help your own children and those of others by being willing to volunteer your time, talents, and hard work to do something about the school's problems. Some school districts have extensive programs in place to seek out, train, and use community volunteers and resources. In a recent year, for example, volunteers in the PALS program contributed more than 190,000 hours of service to the Sarasota County, Florida, school system—the equivalent of 160 full-time staff members!

Even if your school district doesn't have a formal volunteer program, your contributions of time and talent can be very helpful. Begin by asking your child's teacher or principal if there are ways you can help. Consider creating and coordinating a volunteer program if none currently exists. In that way, you not only can contribute your own talents but possibly also tap into a rich resource pool from among your friends, neighbors, and business associates. Begin a list of some possibilities by answering these questions:

- What special interests and activities are really important to me, and how might I be able to share them with youngsters?

- How might some of my skills—artwork, construction, computer work, and the like—be helpful in our school?

- Are there ways that I could help create free time for teachers to plan and conduct special enrichment projects for their students?

- Whom do I know in the community who might have something special they could share with young people? How might I encourage them to do so?

- How can I support the curriculum? What are the major areas of study that will be covered during the year, and what books, videos, films, field trips, special television programs, or other activities would reinforce these studies?

Perhaps the best way to help your school is to inform yourself about education. In Appendix A, we list many books, articles, and other resources that will help you learn more about students' learning characteristics, styles, and strengths, as well as source material about gifted education programs. The more you learn through your own reading and studying, the easier it will be to recognize the good things that are happening in your school and to be alert for possible problems before they become serious.

Your first activities should be orthodox: work through the existing home/school or parent/teacher organizations. A good PTA does more than hold bake sales or arrange car pools, but many PTA members may be hesitant about projects that are described as "gifted" because they frequently associate the term with an exclusive, elitist crowd. Emphasizing the importance of activities that will find and develop the strengths, talents, and interests of *many* students throughout the entire school is a likely way to attract support and enthusiasm.

Some school districts have separate parent organizations that are concerned only with the gifted program. With such groups, you might run into two risks. First, these groups can be viewed by others as elitist and unnecessary competition for other organizations. Second, these groups sometimes *become* elitist—little more than a regular opportunity for a few parents to grind their axes with the school's program or beat the drum for their own children. If you find elitism, fight it. As a general rule, the broader the base of advocacy you can build, the greater impact you can have on the school.

Many states (and provinces in Canada) have statewide (provincial) organizations concerned with gifted education. These groups sometimes limit the breadth of their concerns, focusing too much on traditional IQ-linked approaches to giftedness, but they can be a worthwhile source of information and networking. They are certainly worth investigating, and their annual conferences or workshops can be sources of valuable tips for work accomplished both at home or in school. Local and state organizations often produce newsletters and other publications, and some are actively involved in creating special learning opportunities—after school, on weekends, or over the summer—for children at many age levels. The names and addresses for several of these organizations are in Appendix D. Many of them offer helpful (and often free) literature for parents.

Another way to help support your child's education is to indicate that you value educational success. Talk about the importance of individual learning style and urge respect for the different preferences of others and for the value of critical and creative thinking. Let your child understand that you and the school are working together to help the discovery and development of all the students' best talents and strongest interests. Encourage your child to view learning as enjoyable (even when it's difficult) and to take pride in his or her own accomplishments.

By example, show your child the value of learning in *your* life. Continue to learn and grow, for your own benefit and as evidence to your child that learning and creativity are not merely topics talked about in school, but realities that enrich your family life.

5

Promoting Problem Solving through Creativity and Teamwork at Home

As the world and the changes that are a part of life grow more complex, learning can no longer depend on memorization and recall of information. Today's children will not be able to succeed in the world of the 21st century if they rely only on facts, rules, and procedures they have memorized. Any given field already has more information than anyone can possibly memorize, and our knowledge of the world continues to mushroom as new discoveries are made every day. As knowledge grows, the facts of today may become the errors of tomorrow, and the questions that have been given correct answers will almost certainly be replaced by new and more complex questions.

In 1982, the Education Commission of the United States described skills that should be considered the new bases of education. More complex skills and thinking processes—such as creativity, critical thinking, problem solving, and decision making—are important elements in the emerging picture of what education should be. This doesn't mean that knowledge of basic facts is unimportant; some facts will remain useful no matter what later information is added. But far more relevant for education is a knowledge of how to put facts to use.

Educational leaders and theorists are not alone in beginning to recognize the need for a deeper approach to education. Leaders in business and industry have indicated parallel concerns. A recent survey of the skills that employers expect new employees to bring with them as they enter the workplace shows a strong emphasis on creativity, problem solving, and teamwork.

Guiding children and teenagers in learning and applying better methods for problem solving is an important aspect of bringing out the giftedness in all children. The more skillful and effective young people become as problem solvers, the better they will be prepared to become creatively productive, successful adults.

What Do We Mean by Creative Problem Solving?

Different people use the term "problem solving" in different ways. When we ask groups how they know when they have a problem, the responses usually center on negatives—something's not working, or they feel frustrated or inadequate. When they talk about solving problems, they seem to suggest fixing something or overcoming an obstacle. We believe it's equally important to identify problem solving with great opportunities or challenges. For us, problem solving involves *deliberately using creative techniques to deal with opportunities, challenges, and concerns.* Whenever you need new ideas and a plan to carry them through, you need to become a problem solver.

Creative problem solving involves using a harmonic blend of creative thinking and critical thinking. Three major steps are involved in solving problems productively:

1. Understanding and stating the problem. Make certain that you fully understand the problem you're going to work on. The real problem is often very different from what you imagined it would be.

2. Generating ideas. Work to generate many ideas and especially to find some new ideas that will help you move forward to a solution.

3. Planning for action. Take the ideas you believe are the most promising, analyze and develop them, get others to accept them, and plan specific steps to enable you to carry them out.

All parents can help their children improve their productive thinking. Here are some general guidelines as well as some specific tips you can use in a number of different situations.

A Creative Problem-Solving Approach to Giftedness

Know and Respect Your Child's Unique Characteristics

- Learning style preferences. Both adults and children have their own style for dealing with life's opportunities and challenges. By remaining open to your child's style, you can help with identification of personal challenges and with finding the best way to deal with people, ideas, and experiences.

- Interests. Children develop many interests as they grow up. Problem solving will be more exciting when applied to their interests rather than to the kinds of problems adults think they should be trying to solve.

- **Development and maturity.** All children grow up at different rates—physically, emotionally, and intellectually. The problems that are important to five-year-olds aren't problems at all for teenagers. Listen to your child and note the kinds of things that are talked about or asked about. What topics seem to cause excitement or worry? Be sensitive to the kinds of problems it will be most appropriate to help solve.

- **Strengths.** Children, like adults, are enthusiastic about spending their time and efforts in ways that will bring them success and enjoyment. It is almost always a good strategy to build on the positives instead of pounding away at the negatives.

Know the Ground Rules for Creative Problem Solving

Rule 1. Defer judgment. This is the most basic ground rule for creative thinking. Individuals and groups should always establish this rule from the outset when they are preparing to solve any problem. Criticism can be absolutely deadly to new ideas. This doesn't mean there is never a place for evaluation or critical judgment; each is important in the solution of any problem. But we should separate the generation of ideas from our judgment of them.

When you defer judgment during a brainstorm session, for example, you make a deliberate effort *not* to criticize or praise any new ideas. How many times has your own creativity felt the effects of criticism? You tossed out an idea and others pounced on it, told you it was ridiculous, predicted that it would never work, and reminded you that you couldn't afford it. How did you feel when this happened? Did it cut off the flow of ideas, or begin an argument, or sidetrack your thinking in unproductive ways?

Unqualified praise can be every bit as judgmental as criticism, and just as stifling in its effect on creativity. If you're in a group, what happens after someone comes up with an idea to which the leader or others in the group respond with immediate, all-out enthusiasm? Very often, some members of the group figure the problem is solved and they stop thinking about it. Others may conclude that they could never come up with an idea that good. Still others, trying to get on the bandwagon, start to parrot the idea or offer bland variations on it.

When problem solving, keep these principles in mind:

- Don't criticize *or* praise any ideas.

- Search for, accept, and write down as many ideas as possible. (Strive for quantity; quality will follow.)

- Accept *all* ideas, no matter how wild they might seem. A wild idea from one person may suggest a really unusual but workable idea to someone else, who might not have thought of it otherwise.

- Be a "hitchhiker." Look for combinations of ideas, and try to make new connections with the ideas of others.

Rule 2. Use affirmative judgment. This is the other side of the deferred judgment coin. After you have deferred judgment and generated a number of ideas, the time for critical thinking begins. *Critical thinking is not the same as criticism.* For many people, criticism means going on the attack, giving all the reasons for opposing or disliking an idea. True critical thinking involves making a careful, thorough analysis of several ideas, looking at their strengths and weaknesses, and trying to refine or strengthen promising ideas to make them as good as possible. Observation, logical analysis, and deliberation are used to compare and evaluate ideas fairly and completely before reaching a conclusion or decision. Remember these simple rules for affirmative judgment:

- **Be fair and deliberate.** Good decisions don't just happen—you *make* them. Decision making, as much as any other skill, can be improved by working slowly and deliberately.

- **Stay on course.** A ship's captain needs to follow navigation charts carefully and keep a watchful eye on the vessel's course. In the same way, good thinkers and problem solvers should stay focused on their goals and objectives.

- **Consider novelty.** Solving a problem calls on you to be receptive to new ideas and fresh possibilities. Don't be too quick to reject ideas you hadn't considered until now.

Encourage Curiosity and Exploration

Good problem solving comes from having good problems to solve. You can help your child find opportunities to practice problem solving in a variety of ways. Some of these include:

- Encouraging hobbies, collections, and scrapbooks.

- Supporting participation in youth groups, clubs, and outside lessons.

- Making family field trips to museums, galleries, zoos, and historical places.

- Suggesting outdoor activities, camping, and travel.

- Making family time for reading (independently and aloud).

- Using computers together (and not just for Nintendo games).

- Attending concerts, plays, films, and exhibits together.

- Involving youngsters in discussion and dialogue about events, ideas, and experiences.

- Using television and videos constructively—monitoring programs and rentals and discussing them together.

- Learning from sports.

The last item deserves some comment. Many parents spend huge amounts of time, energy, and money helping their children pursue team sports. They buy uniforms and equipment, go to practices, attend meetings and games, and cheer until they're hoarse. Hockey-playing children are transported to rinks by their parents close to midnight or at the crack of dawn. We wish that parents were as enthusiastic and participative about other kinds of talents and the activities that go with them.

Don't Suffocate Children with Helpfulness

Children need to do things for themselves, to work on problems in ways that encourage them to generate ideas, to choose promising possibilities, and to develop their own action plans. By carrying out their plans, they find out for themselves what works and what doesn't. It may be easier or more convenient for you to simply tell your child what to do, but not nearly as much learning will take place that way. Besides, there will come a time when the last thing your child will want to do is what you have suggested. Start early to allow independent generation and analysis of ideas.

If your child has never learned how to solve problems effectively, encouragement to solve a problem alone isn't helpful and may seem to condone careless thinking or unproductive efforts.

Even when you don't tell your child what the problem's answer is, you might offer to help in solving the problem by being a guide or a resource for ideas.

Give Children Challenging Opportunities

You can prepare your child to be a good problem solver by providing a safe environment for exploring, raising questions, and growing in new directions. Here are some important tips for creating a supportive environment.

- **Respect and encourage questions.** Parents would do well to take to heart the maxim "There's no such thing as a dumb question—except for the ones that didn't get asked." You don't have to know the answers to all the questions, but you can treat all questions with respect by guiding the search for answers. For example, ask your child where answers to a question might be found, then help identify resources such as books, magazines, videos, or appropriate people.

- **Don't punish errors.** When youngsters try to solve problems independently, they are certain to make mistakes. Discuss the errors, analyze them, and talk about ways to avoid them in the future, but don't equate errors with failure.

- **Love your child for being, not just for doing.** Children should not begin to feel they are loved only when they're doing well. Love your child unconditionally, then help with growing and learning to solve problems.

- **Don't overprogram; allow time for reflection.** Everyone needs some quiet, solitary time for nothing in particular, and some people need more than others. Don't arrange so many activities that your child loses this precious time.

Guiding Children to Become Better Problem Solvers

Setting a good foundation is only the starting point for creative problem solving. To build on that foundation, you'll need to help your child learn (and practice) some specific techniques. Don't forget that you can use these techniques yourself—in fact, it's best if you use them together as a family.

Teach and Use Tools for Generating and Analyzing Ideas

Effective problem solving involves both creative thinking and critical thinking, not just one or the other. You can help your children to learn and apply several useful strategies for both types of thinking.

When you are generating new ideas, your *creative thinking* is at work. We noted earlier that creative thinking can be seen in several different ways: fluency (the production of many ideas), flexibility (the ability to look at situations from different points of view), originality (the production of unique or unusual possibilities), and elaboration (the refinement of ideas by adding details that make the original ideas more complete or interesting).

The following techniques will promote creating thinking:

- *Brainstorming.* For an open-ended question, list as many ideas as you can. Write all the ideas down so that you can examine them more carefully and critically at a later time. For example, ask your child to think of all the things that might be seen at a shopping mall, or the various activities that can be done indoors on a rainy day.

- *Product improvement.* This technique involves generating ideas for improving common objects to make them better, more interesting, or more useful. For example, how would your child improve a fork or a toothbrush, or design the perfect bathtub?

- *"What if . . . ?"* Creative thinking can often result when you begin to wonder "What would happen if I tried this?" You can use any number of what-if questions to involve your child in generating ideas. What would happen if it always rained on Saturday? If students and teachers could choose what times and seasons they wanted to go to school? If every car in the world were purple?

- *Random combinations.* New ideas often come from looking at something that has nothing to do with the problem and discovering a new connection by force-fitting things together in new ways. When you're stuck and can't think of new ideas, try making a list of random objects: the first three things you see when you look around the room or take a walk, or all the things mentioned on one page of the Yellow Pages, for instance. Then take each of those objects, one at a time, and try to use it to trigger some new problem-solving ideas. Be sure that the objects are a random collection. If you try to pick things you think will fit the problem, you won't be able to stretch yourself to find new connections.

  As an example, you and your ten-year-old are trying to think of ideas for a birthday party. You look at a supermarket ad in your local newspaper and you pick the first couple of objects you see. A head of lettuce might suggest a costume party in which everyone comes as a favorite (or least favorite) fruit or vegetable; or you could use construction paper or other materials to make vegetables (or flowers) as decorations; or everyone could bring something that is an ingredient for a huge salad that is made and eaten at the party. A box of frozen carrots and peas might suggest a theme: everyone could bring something green and orange to the party; or party favors could be made using green vegetables and tooth-picks; or a team game could be organized around the theme of Carrots versus Peas.

Your *critical thinking* is at work when you make decisions or when you analyze and evaluate ideas that you have heard or seen from others. Critical thinking can also be expressed in several other ways: observing carefully and thoroughly, think-ing through analogies, comparing and contrasting, arranging ideas or objects into categories or sequences, recognizing the advantages and limitations of ideas, judging ideas using specific criteria, and reaching logical conclusions through inductive or deductive reasoning.

Some of the techniques you can teach your child to promote critical thinking include:

- *Improving observation skills.* Take a common object—an orange, for instance—and try to make as many different observations about it as you can. Remember to use all five senses. Or solve the puzzles that often appear on the comics page of newspapers—given two very similar pictures, you have to find ways in which the pictures are different.

- *Comparing, contrasting, and using analogies.* To help your child learn to reason by analogy, encourage making sim-ple comparisons and contrasts. How are two objects alike? Are they alike in several different ways? How do they differ? For example, you could compare computers and pencils. They are alike because we use both to record our thoughts and to work with words, numbers, and pictures. They are different because a pencil doesn't need an operator's manual, or because the computer lets you rearrange your words before they appear on paper, and so forth.

From simple comparisons and contrasts, you can move to analogies. To continue with the computer/ pencil example, you could ask your child to think of two other things that are related to each other in the same way (or nearly the same way) that a computer is to a pencil. As it is often phrased in workbooks, a computer is to a pencil as WHAT is to WHAT? An answer might be: a computer is to a pencil as a car is to a bicycle. The bicycle and the pencil are less complicated means of performing certain activities (going for a ride, and writing) than are the computer and the car. The bicycle (or pencil) takes up a lot less space than a car (or computer) and is much cheaper to buy.

- *Categorizing.* Given a group of separate objects, can you form groups that share common attributes? Or, given a list of items that are all part of the same group, can you tell what makes them members of that category? As an example, give this list: bed, toaster, nightstand, refrigerator, pillow, blanket, dishwasher, stove. Have your child divide them into two groups (most naturally, things found in the kitchen and things found in the bedroom). Of the items found in each room, which ones have similar characteristics? Try another list: sausage, pepperoni, onions, mushrooms, olives, cheese, tomato sauce. Can your child find the feature that relates all of these things?

- *Sequencing.* This skill involves the ability to recognize an appropriate arrangement of events. For example, you might list the things your child does to get ready for school in the morning (walk out the door, eat breakfast, get dressed, brush teeth, and so on). What's the order in which they get done properly?

- *Balancing advantages and limitations.* A person who uses constructive critical thinking knows how to examine ideas in a thorough, fair, and balanced way—to look at an idea closely before accepting or rejecting it. A useful strategy is the A-L-U technique, in which a new idea is examined in three ways:

  —Advantages: What might be the advantages of the idea? What's good about it?

  —Limitations: What are the boundaries of the idea? Instead of stating them in a negative way, express them as "how to" or "how might we" statements—not "You can't afford to buy a computer" but "How can you find the resources to buy a computer?"

  —Unique potentials: What is unique or different about this idea? What else might it lead to or pave the way for?

- *Evaluating ideas.* When you have many possibilities to consider in making a decision, it may be helpful to think about the criteria that need to be met and then evaluate your options carefully, using those criteria. For example, suppose your teenager is applying for a first summer job. Together, you can compile a list of criteria that might be important to the youngster by answering the following questions:

  —What kind of training will be offered, or is previous experience in that type of employment necessary?

  —How many hours per day or week will be required?

  —Are weekend or night hours required?

—What will it cost to go to and from work?

—Are food and beverages easily available and how much will they cost?

—What is the minimum salary that will be accepted?

—What safety factors should be considered in the place or neighborhood of employment?

—To what extent will experience in this field help with future employment?

—Is a creative or perfunctory assignment preferred?

—Are benefits important at this stage?

—Will there be opportunities to invest or save money?

—Is there the potential for growth or for periodic employment during future summers in that company?

—Is there a real interest in eventually becoming involved in this type of business?

—Is special clothing or a uniform required for this job?

—Will there be an opportunity for skill development?

—Does it involve services for others? If so, what kind of services?

—Does the youngster have the abilities or strengths that match this job's requirements?

Be Problem Solvers Together

Good problem solving is more than being able to use a number of tools or strategies for creative and critical thinking. The skills and activities we've described so far are only the building blocks for creative problem solving. To be most effective in using them, you may want to incorporate them into some additional, family activities that will help your child and you to solve many different kinds of problems.

Earlier in the chapter, we described the three general components of creative problem solving: understanding the problem, generating ideas, and planning for action. The next section identifies several specific activities that will help you guide your child in problem solving.

General Tips for Using Creative Problem Solving at Home

The principles we've been describing can be used successfully at home, at school, at work, or nearly anywhere else. For more than three decades, research and real-life applications have shown that creative problem solving can be used in many different kinds of problems and for all ages. Here are a few additional tips to help you make it useful in your family.

- *Take—MAKE—time.* At this point, you might want to ask: "Do you really expect us to spend hours making lists and coming up with ideas every time a little problem comes up?" Yes. If the problem is important enough to you, take the time to work it out. It takes no more time to work through a problem effectively than it does to plunge into it and then have to go back and start over. An early industrialist is supposed to have complained: "There's never enough time to do it right, but there's always time enough to do it over." Keep in mind that different problems will require different amounts of time to work out: there are two-minute problems and two-year problems. Find the time that each problem warrants. Remember that you can always work on the problem step-by-step, over a period of several days. You don't have to solve everything in one sitting.

- *Establish ground rules and stick with them.* Before you begin working on a problem, review the ground rules, especially the deferred judgment and affirmative judgment principles. Be sure everyone understands them and agrees to follow them.

- *Accept your children as full participants.* In a family session, everyone's ideas should have the same weight. If your children feel their ideas are not heard or respected—that adults are only using the process to push their own ideas—they will quickly lose interest.

- *Develop a plan and follow it.* To make creative problem solving work, don't approach it as an exercise or activity. Use it with real problems for which you want solutions. When you reach your plan of action, carry it out.

- *Write down all ideas.* Get a *large* sketching pad or a lecturer's display pad from a local stationery store or an art or office supply outlet. Tape sheets up on a solid surface where everyone can see them. As you proceed through the creative problem-solving process, write down all the ideas suggested for each step, using a marker that's easy to read. Number the ideas on each sheet, and number the pages as you go. (You may want to refer back to them as you move along.) When one sheet is full, move it aside but tape it where it can still be seen; don't hide it. Work right on the sheets, all the way through to writing out your plan of action.

- *Talk about what you have done together.* When you've finished a problem-solving session and all the sheets of paper are still up on the walls, look back at the process and talk about what you've done, how everyone reacted to it, and how you can improve it the next time. This "debriefing" is an important part of the learning process.

- *Be sure you know what everyone is doing.* In a problem-solving session, it's helpful if everyone in the group knows who *owns* the problem. The owner (client is another good term) is the person who will be responsible for carrying out the plan of action. Other members of the group are like a think tank for the client. Their role is to come up with ideas that the client wouldn't have thought of alone. One person in the group can act as the *facilitator,* assuming responsibility for guiding the group through the process. (The facilitator doesn't have to be a parent.)

- *Keep the tone light and enjoyable.* Creative problem solving shouldn't be a test or a formal lesson. It should be fast-paced and enjoyable for everyone involved. Keep the focus on working together to move toward a solution to the problem, but leave room for some fun as well.

Summary: Creative Problem Solving and Giftedness

One of the most important messages we want to convey in this book is that recognizing each child's unique style and helping children learn to be productive thinkers will pave the way for any schoolchild to realize the fullest benefits of his or her talents. Bringing out the best—the giftedness—in every child is largely a matter of knowing and respecting each one's unique style and being able to use strategies that will promote productive thinking and creative problem solving.

When people use their unique style to find ways to excel, when they apply the tools of creative and critical thinking, they can discover opportunities for significant accomplishments— the level of achievements that the world knows as gifts.

In the following chapter, we'll suggest practical activities and projects to stimulate giftedness.

6

Practical Activities to Stimulate Giftedness

Getting children involved in projects and activities that will help them to develop verbal, analytic, and creative capacities is an essential component of nurturing their giftedness. An infinite number of such projects and resources is possible; we've included a sampling to help you and your child get started. Use the ideas we've suggested as a basis for creating your own activities together. Creating new, interesting projects and activities with your child will stimulate other creative thinking.

Realizing the prevalence of television in our culture today, we've devoted considerable attention to using television in creative, productive ways. Why not make the best of it and treat it as a tool for bringing out giftedness?

Sample Activities

Your child can have fun, compete, and find rewards in activities that encourage learning. The activities suggested in this section are grouped for the development of particular skills but are not limited to those skills. Many of the games and activities help to develop multiple skills and have been classified according to their predominant teaching purpose, not their only one.

Verbal Skills

- **Vocabulary Words.** If your youngster is auditory, teach new words by speaking them. Dramatize each word and explain its meaning. Give an example of how it might be used in a sentence, then have your child repeat the word and use it in a sentence. When this step is mastered, spell the word. Help your youngster find the word in a newspaper and perhaps even cut it out, paste it onto an index card, and illustrate it with crayons. The child can create a collection of these cards, and keep them in a New Word file (a shoe box works well).

- **Word Parts.** If your youngster is primarily visual, print new words in black on a colored sheet of paper, then in white on a black piece of paper. Repeat the spelling and point to each letter as you say it. Subdivide the word into syllables or smaller words or letter groups. Ask your child to look at these smaller groups and try to memorize the letters in their correct sequence. Make up a story about the word—or each part—to emphasize the various sections or shorter words inside the larger one. Ask your child to try and write the word without look-ing at it. Examples: *Ele-ph-ant, car-t, some-one, hip-po-pot-a-mus.* Say each part, and use it in a sentence or story. Find the word on a page of a book or in the newspaper. A starting point can be the new words encountered in a story you're reading together.

- **Sand Tracing.** Empty the contents of a small bag of sand (or salt or sugar) into a flat pan. Encourage your child to trace the letters of a new word in the sand (or salt or sugar) by looking at the printed word and copying its letters. Then see if your child can write the letters without looking at the word. If so, work on spelling the word without looking or writing.

- **Water Writing.** Ask your child to dip a finger into a cup of water and then write a word on a small chalkboard without looking at the printed version. It can be fun for a child to watch the word evaporate, "see" the word with eyes closed, and then write it down.

- **Letter Box.** Using thick paper or index cards, cut out freehand letters of the alphabet (or trace them from block-letter sheets sold at many art supply stores). Place all the letters into an empty box and ask your child to find those needed to spell a specific word by feeling each of the letters (not looking at them) and selecting the correct ones. When all the letters have been found, the child then can place them into the correct sequence to spell the word. (You can purchase premade letters commercially, but it may be a better learning experience to have your child cut out the letters or help you do it. Make more than one cutout of vowels and popular consonants like s, d, t, c, and r.

- **Cloth Alphabet.** Cut alphabet letters from fabric, using different colors for vowels and consonants.

- **Macaroni Spelling.** Keep a jar of uncooked alphabet macaroni or a box of alphabet cereal available for spelling. Ask your child to find the letters in a word and glue them onto cardboard, creating a three-dimensional spelling list. Alternately, use flat, narrow, uncooked noodles. The child can form large letters on paper or cardboard by using several noodle pieces for each letter.

- **Pudding Spelling.** A young child might enjoy tracing letters and words in soft gelatin or warm chocolate pudding, with fingers or a small spoon. Pouring milk into the "letters" in the pudding will reinforce the visual image created. When the word is spelled correctly, the reward can be permission to eat the dessert.

- **The Critic.** If your child can read with comprehension, suggest a review of a book, movie, television show, or video as though he or she were a professional critic. The review should discuss the reasons for liking or disliking the book or program chosen.

- **Illustrated Dictionary.** Your child will enjoy making an illustrated looseleaf dictionary for new vocabulary words. Add to the dictionary each time a new word is learned. Each word should have a page of its own so that new words can be added in alphabetical order.

Active Participation

- **Floor Games.** Encourage your child to create floor games using old shower curtains, large plastic rectangles, bed sheets, or flattened-out cardboard cartons. With any of these and a little glue, felt, and pictures, the products can be map games, treasure hunts, science puzzles, math adventures, or mystery-solving events. Add a few spinners with numbers, dice, or sequenced cards to direct players to move and respond to the next question, and let your child's imagination do the rest.

- **Question and Answer Darts.** You can create "relay" games in math, spelling, science, and other subjects by using safe Velcro™ darts and a board that is covered with questions written on index cards. Have your child and friends line up in teams. Give each team a different colored marker. Have one of the children (or you) keep score. Each player throws a dart, runs to the board to answer the question hit, removes the card and writes the answer on it, gives it to the scorekeeper, and then races back to give the dart and marker to the next player on the team. After all the questions are answered, the cards are read aloud to reveal the winning team: the one with the best time *and* the most correct answers. Because all players learn the correct answers, everyone wins.

- **Cup Toss.** On index cards, write questions with varying degrees of difficulty on one side of the card and the answers on the other. Separate the cards into three piles: easy, medium, and hard. Have your children and friends toss paper clips, ping pong balls, or similar objects into plastic cups with the numbers 1, 2, and 3 marked on them. For each toss that lands in the cup marked 1, the player gets to answer a question from the easy pile of cards and scores one point; for every toss into the cup marked 2, a correct answer to the medium set of questions gets 2 points, and so on. Have teams or individual players keep score and see who gets the most answers right and the highest score. Expect some objections to what are given as "easy" questions.

- **Poster Making.** Using illustrations and words clipped from newspapers and magazines, have your child make a poster that illustrates or advertises the most interesting thing he or she has learned that week.

- **Model Making.** Give your child clay, soap, or wood to make a model of an object that he or she finds interesting or attractive. Cars, flowers, people, animals, or something very unusual may be the products.

- **Murals.** Allow your child to draw or paint a mural to illustrate something especially fascinating. Talk about how murals have been used in the past to show people specific historical events. What events would artists show on a mural of today? One roll of white wallcovering taped across a reachable wall space will provide several "murals."

- **Dioramas.** Using a shoebox or other cardboard box turned on its side, help your child to build a diorama to depict an important event or scene. This box can contain scenes of dinosaurs, farmlands, cities, or any topic of study or interest.

- **Songwriting.** Your child can write a song about something learned or experienced, or a place visited. New lyrics can be written for a song that is already known.

- **Time Line.** Make a random list of important dates and events in history. Using a felt tip pen, have your child draw a time line across a long sheet of paper and fill in the dates on the line, in chronological order. Pictures or drawings that depict important historical events can be added.

- **Library Trip.** Search through libraries or museums for original manuscripts, old page proofs or book jackets, first editions of books, taped interviews with authors or other interesting persons in the community, autographs of writers, or any other documentation related to a topic being studied. If the material cannot be taken to school, organize a small group trip to visit the library or museum where the item was found.

- **Food Clippings.** Using the Sunday newspaper, have your child find and cut out pictures of nutritious foods, paste them onto cardboard or heavy construction paper to make charts, and prepare a display of examples of balanced breakfasts and lunches that could be eaten in school. Similar charts can be made for dinners at home.

- **Good Breakfasts.** Encourage your child to investigate and explain the importance of eating a full and nutritious breakfast and to compare the vitamins and minerals listed in favorite breakfast foods—especially how much sugar they contain.

- **Learning about Health.** Explain one aspect (such as fat or cholesterol) of the health and well-being of adults who are overweight. Ask your child to make a list of foods high in cholesterol, using the food value lists on packages investigated during a supermarket trip.

- **Debates.** Using magazine articles, newspapers, and books from the library, have an older child investigate a current news topic of interest. Then, with family or the child's friends, organize two sides of a debate or panel discussion on the topic. If the topic is controversial, allow the various opinions or viewpoints to be offered.

- **Library Research.** Show your child how to search your library's card catalog and the periodical index, and list all of the books and articles concerning a topic he or she selects—dolls, sports, dinosaurs, famous people. The possibilities are endless.

- **Growing Seeds.** Buy your child some seeds (radishes or lima beans are a good start) to plant in two plastic cups filled with soil. Give one water and sunlight and keep the other in a closet or dark place without water. Wait for two weeks, then let your child observe the progress of each.

- **Plants and Flowers.** Take your child to visit a park, a neighbor's garden, or a florist, and ask the people there to talk about how they take care of different plants and flowers. You might want to suggest such a visit to the teacher for your child's class.

- **Colored Celery.** Let your child put a stalk of celery into a cup of water that contains food coloring and observe what happens to the celery. Discuss what "capillary action" is and why it worked on the celery.

- **Seed Bags.** Have your child carefully break or cut open different fruits, remove the seeds, and put each kind into a small plastic bag. Make a seed chart by first attaching the bags to a piece of cardboard. Then ask your child to cut out pictures of fruit from magazines or supermarket circulars (or draw them) and match them up with the correct seed bags.

- **Tree Pictures.** Your child can observe certain trees and draw colored pictures of what each one looks like in each of the four seasons; or, using magazine pictures, cut and paste tree pictures from each season onto construction paper and correctly label the time of year for each tree.

- **Scrapbook.** A scrapbook can be made about a favorite topic, using pictures and articles from magazines and newspapers.

- **Book Covers.** Let your child dress up like a favorite character from a book, a television show, or a movie. Take a photo for use on a make-believe book cover or poster that the child designs.

Imaginative Development

- **Board Games.** Your child can help cover old or worn-out board games with white Con-tact,™ and invent new games by drawing on the white surface with colored markers. Clear Con-tact stripped on over the new games will protect them for years to come.

- **Historical Costumes.** Help your child to imagine items of clothing that might have been worn by people or fictional characters read about or studied. Keep in mind the country and climate the character lived in, the historical time of the character's lifespan, what the character did for a living, and so on. If you can, try to assemble a costume, adapting old clothes from around the house, old curtains or drapes, or crepe paper.

- **New Recipes.** Brainstorm new types of food, recipes, and meals. Obtain a consensus on which ones to try. You may want to use cookbooks, magazines, and newspapers for ideas. Or, choose a country, research its national foods, and have your child help you prepare one of its dishes.

- **Menu Contest.** Hold a contest to develop menus for the most attractive, nutritious meals.

- **Monthly Calendar.** Make a calendar for the coming month, illustrating all the family's special days and any holidays. For example, have your child draw a party hat or cake for birthdays, a heart for Valentine's Day, a pumpkin for Halloween, and so forth. Do this for several months, to teach that there are different events and numbers of days in certain months.

- **Rhyming Poems.** Ask your child to make up a poem using rhyming words at the end of each line. For example:

> I saw a big cat.
> That cat sure was fat.
> It saw me and ran
> Behind a red van.

The poem can then be illustrated.

- **Travel Agent.** Your child can pretend to be a travel agent and prepare a travel lecture about an interesting place to visit and the people who live there. The lecture should include the food the people eat, how they dress, and the language they speak; what kind of climate the country or state has, its geographic location, and so on. Try to find magazine clippings to illustrate the travel lecture.

- **Paper Movie.** A "movie reel" can be made by drawing a series of pictures on a long sheet of paper fastened by two rollers (you can use empty bathroom tissue rollers). A script or story can be written as a "sound track."

- **Story Endings.** Ask your child to write or tell a different ending to a story you read or a show or movie you watched together. In what unusual ways could the story have evolved? How might your child have liked it to end?

- **Maps and Charts.** Using a large piece of cardboard or construction paper, help your child to make a map or chart representing facts and information gathered about a specific topic or place of interest. For example, make a chart listing the various countries that speak a particular language (e.g., Spanish).

- **Interesting People.** In writing, or on a cassette tape, let your child describe an interesting person or character who has been met or learned about. What makes this person special? What traits or skills of the person would your child like to have? In what ways could those skills be learned?

- **Puppet Shows.** Make a large diorama as described above, but remove or make a flap out of the "ceiling" panel. Construct puppets for a show in the diorama.

- **Crossword Puzzle.** Familiarize your child with the crossword concept through children's crossword books or by working together on a crossword puzzle from your local paper. Using spelling, reading, or vocabulary words, have your child make up a crossword puzzle and give it to a friend to solve.

- **Imaginary Letters.** After you read a story together, ask your child what an imaginary letter from one character to another might have said. Or, what might two familiar people or family members have written to each other if they had both lived at the time and place of the story?

- **Tall Tales.** Many children love to make up tall tales. Tape-record some of the tales created, or have your child write them down and illustrate them.

- **News Reporter.** Pretending to be a news reporter, your child can write a news story, editorial, or special column for the school or class newspaper (or just for you), explaining a current news event or topic. Emphasize trying to be objective in reporting the facts of the story, but sharing his or her own views as well.

- **The "Human" Tree.** Ask your child, using mime and/or a script, to dramatize how a tree might feel in winter, spring, summer, and fall, by playing the role of a favorite tree.

Writing Skills

- **Daily Journal.** Have your child keep a journal of daily activities, ideas, and impressions, and illustrate it with drawings or pictures from magazines. The journal can be a notebook with a decorated cover, or looseleaf sheets of paper tied together with brightly colored yarn and covered with decorated construction paper.

- **Rewriting Stories.** Ask an older child to rewrite a story he or she has read, simplifying the vocabulary for a younger brother, sister, or neighbor. When rewriting the story, the child should try to remember to use only words that the younger child can read and understand.

- **Scriptwriting.** Encourage your child to write a script for a short radio or television program, to be staged for family and friends. Adding some commercials, especially for fictitious products, can increase the fun.

- **Diaries.** Ask your child to keep a diary of make-believe experiences as if they had been lived through in a past period of history or were being lived at some time in the future.

Using Television
to Promote Creative Thinking

Virtually every household in the United States has one television set and many have two or more. It has been estimated that the average set is on between six and seven hours each day. This means that, by the time your child reaches the age of sixteen, he or she will have spent about fifteen thousand hours perched in front of the tube, at least four thousand more hours than will have been spent in a classroom. If you can improve the quality of your child's television viewing so that it includes more programs on world events, fine films, nature, history, drama, and sporting events, these hours can nurture and expand your youngster's view of the world.

One book we have found useful in this regard is *The A.C.T. Guide to Children's Television* by Evelyn Kaye. The book assesses various types of children's programs and gives a kind of "boob tube how-to" guide as to what to watch, what to miss, what to change, and how to decide. The National Association for Better Broadcasting (NABB) offers guidelines for evaluating programs in its list of questions that will help you assess what you watch. Each question offers a standard by which to judge a program and some examples of positive and negative aspects of the standard.

We've based the Television Standards Worksheet in Figure 6.1 on the NABB guidelines. Use the Worksheet to guide your children in thinking about the television programs they watch and distinguishing between desirable and undesirable programming. For each of the standards on the Worksheet, you and your child should write in specific examples of whether and how the standard was applied. If you have a VCR, it may be helpful to videotape programs and review sections on which there is disagreement. This interactive viewing will not only help you and your child to distinguish good from bad television, but will help to sharpen your family's critical skills regarding the medium in general.

You can use the behavioral traits checklist in Figure 6.2 to sharpen your child's television viewing skills and increase his or her critical ability to judge between right and wrong in real life. Using scenarios that occur in television shows, ask what your child would have done, or what the television character should have done, in a particular situation.

Using the checklist, focus on particular traits and note how certain characters are presented in a given program. How many times does a particular character exhibit anger, compassion, intelligence? Do the women in the script differ significantly from the men in this regard? What do the results tell you about television in general? This critical approach can be used for watching films and plays as well.

Figure 6.1   Television Standards Worksheet

Television Program   _____

Date   _____

Channel   _____

Main Theme   _____

	Program Qualities	
Standard	Desirable	Undesirable
Intended Audience Appeals to the audience for whom it was intended.	Gives information or entertainment related to authentic, real-life situations or viewers' interests.	Remains dull, unchallenging, not related to viewers' experiences or interests; exaggerates situations beyond believability.
a. _____	a. _____	a. _____
b. _____	b. _____	b. _____
c. _____	c. _____	c. _____
Entertainment Value Meets people's needs for entertainment and action.	Provides wholesome adventure, humor, fantasy, suspense.	Has an unnecessary emphasis on cruelty and violence; loud, crude, or vulgar.
a. _____	a. _____	a. _____
b. _____	b. _____	b. _____
c. _____	c. _____	c. _____

Figure 6.1 *(continued)*

| Standard | Program Qualities | |
	Desirable	Undesirable
Human Values Encourages worthwhile ideals, values, and beliefs (family life, etc.).	Upholds acceptable standards of behavior; promotes democratic and spiritual values, respect for law, decency, service.	Glamorizes crime, indecency, intolerance, greed, cruelty; encourages only material success, false standards of vanity, intemperance, immorality.
a. _____	a. _____	a. _____
b. _____	b. _____	b. _____
c. _____	c. _____	c. _____
Constructive Orientation Stimulates constructive activities.	Promotes interests, skills, hobbies; encourages desire to learn more, to do something constructive, to be creative, to solve problems, to work and live with others.	Emphasizes violence and crime; solves problems by brute force, or resolves situations by chance rather than by logical story development.
a. _____	a. _____	a. _____
b. _____	b. _____	b. _____
c. _____	c. _____	c. _____

(continued)

Figure 6.1 *(continued)*

Standard	Program Qualities	
	Desirable	Undesirable
Artistic Value Displays true artistic qualities.	Offers skillful production values: music, script, acting, direction, artwork, sets, sound effects, photography.	Has been poorly produced; confusing; hard to follow; action too fast or too slow; poor sound or picture quality.
a. _____	a. _____	a. _____
b. _____	b. _____	b. _____
c. _____	c. _____	c. _____
Commercial Content Has acceptable commercials.	Presents program breaks with courtesy and good taste; reasonably brief; in harmony with content and sound volume of program.	Offends by being too loud, too frequent, deceptive; poor taste in content and treatment.
a. _____	a. _____	a. _____
b. _____	b. _____	b. _____
c. _____	c. _____	c. _____

Figure 6.1 *(continued)*

Standard	Program Qualities	
	Desirable	Undesirable
Depiction of Women Presents an accurate and unbiased view of girls' and women's social roles and personal traits.	Depicts girls and women fairly, showing strengths and weaknesses, and appropriate aspirations equal to those of men; valued traits presented as desirable for both, with warmth and love, between a couple and toward people in general, the traits of both sexes.	Characterizes females as scheming, inferior, deceptive, brainless, frivolous, powerless, undignified, in lesser roles, service-oriented, valued only for attraction and appearance, absent from the plot (without historical justification), or decorative without significance.
a. _____	a. _____	a. _____
b. _____	b. _____	b. _____
c. _____	c. _____	c. _____
Depiction of Minorities Gives an objective representation of minority populations and ethnic groups, with acceptance and proper respect for their right to preserve their traditions within the structure of the larger, multicultural society.	Places minority characters in any current role, place, or situation that may be filled by any member of the predominant society.	Limits minority characters to substandard social status; emphasizes or criticizes subcultural preferences; uses speech, dress, economic status, or racial/ national/religious identification as source of ridicule.
a. _____	a. _____	a. _____
b. _____	b. _____	b. _____
c. _____	c. _____	c. _____

Figure 6.2   Behavioral Traits Checklist

Trait	Number of Times Trait Is Observed	
	Male Characters	Female Characters
Compassion	_____	_____
Anger	_____	_____
Aggression	_____	_____
Cowardice	_____	_____
Incompetence	_____	_____
Dishonesty	_____	_____
Violence	_____	_____
Hysteria	_____	_____
Jealousy	_____	_____
Selfishness	_____	_____
Discrimination/Racism	_____	_____
Vanity	_____	_____
Tenderness	_____	_____
Bravery	_____	_____
Competence	_____	_____
Intelligence	_____	_____
Honesty	_____	_____
Humor	_____	_____
Supportiveness	_____	_____
Altruism	_____	_____

These activities can help your child develop critical viewing skills, but the time spent watching television should still be limited to one or two hours a day. Television watching is essentially passive, and children learn best from active involvement. These practical ideas and guidelines for television viewing should help you to invent other educational activities that can provide opportunities for growth, creativity, productivity, and the continuing development of the unique individual gifts of your child.

7

Identifying Your Child's Learning Style

The concept of learning style encompasses a child's environmental, emotional, social, physiological, and global or analytical learning preferences. If you know your child's learning style strengths and preferences, you will be able to help maximize his or her potential for giftedness. A parent doesn't often have control over the learning environment, but knowing your child's preferences will enable you to work more closely with teachers to enhance your child's learning.

At present, there is no research-based test for identifying the learning styles of *preschool* children. You can only observe your child as he or she begins to concentrate on cognitive tasks. Until preschoolers enter kindergarten, simple observation and questioning are the best ways to understand their learning style strengths. Watch how your child approaches difficult information. Experiment with a variety of resources for teaching challenging material, and determine which seem to be most advantageous for your child.

If you'd like immediate insight into the learning style of a child (in grades 3 through 12), you can use the Learning Style Questionnaire (Figure 7.1), which has been shown to be accurate and consistent for the same schoolchildren over time. Complete the questionnaire with your children; there's no need to complete it in one sitting. Administer the questionnaire by asking your child to answer "true" or "false" to the various statements. Be sure to let your child know that there is no "wrong" or "right" answer to these statements and that the questionnaire differs from a test given in school.

The questionnaire will show you how your child learns most easily and how to create an environment best suited to your child's learning needs. Some elements of learning style gradually change over time, but we have found that when one particular element is important to a child (lighting, for instance), that element will remain stable over several years and even for a lifetime. Less important traits are likely to change over the course of two or more years in relation to the child's experience, maturation, and motivation. As your child progresses through school, we encourage you to share his or her learning style profiles with teachers. Very rarely in educational situations can you work to create an *ideal* learning environment for your child, but you can become a partner in unlocking your child's giftedness by working with educators to trying to create optimal learning conditions that maximize your child's potential for giftedness.

Taking the Questionnaire

It is helpful for children to understand the importance of learning styles before they begin the Learning Style Questionnaire. They can then think carefully before answering questions about how they learn. Appendix C contains information on supplemental storybooks developed at The Center for the Study of Learning and Teaching Styles which, though not necessary for administering the questionnaire, may be of use to parents in explaining the concept of learning styles to children. When you discuss the notion of learning styles with your child, emphasize that there are no "right" or "wrong" styles or "correct" answers to the learning style statements.

Your child can be given this questionnaire in writing, orally, on tape, or in any combination of these media. Again, the questionnaire need not be answered in one sitting, but can be completed at intervals that are convenient to both you and your child.

For children who do not read fluently or who are too young to fully understand the statements, administer the questionnaire by discussing each statement personally with the child. The one-to-one communication that develops as you question your child about learning preferences often provides new insights into the child's way of learning that may not be attainable by any other means.

Scoring and Interpreting Your Child's Questionnaire

When the questionnaire has been completed, all of the "true" and "false" answers in each category should be checked against the scoring key that follows each section. When answers are fairly evenly divided for any one learning style element (showing no strong preference), that element may just not be *important* to your child. You will find that, although there are many elements of learning style, very few children shows strong preferences with regard to every element. For some children, only two or three elements are important; other children have as many as ten or more. As with the statements themselves, there are no "wrongs" or "rights" here. Each child learns in his or her unique way.

Comments on your child's learning style preferences in each category should be noted on the Learning Style Profile

(Figure 7.2) and should be used (if possible) to individualize your child's instructional program at school. As stated earlier, it is useful to share your child's learning style preferences with educators. Research has shown that most students are able to identify how they learn, learn better when taught through their learning style strengths, and are more receptive and cooperative when permitted to learn through their learning style preferences.

A final reminder: no learning style is either "good" or "bad." Each merely provides insight into how a given person is most likely to learn new and difficult information. One student will need a quiet place to concentrate. Another will function better with soft music in the background than with absolute quiet. Still others will prefer murmuring voices and, generally speaking, will find background noises acceptable. Such preferences may seem odd to you; many adults have been taught that *everybody* needs quiet. That assumption, we now know, is sometimes wrong. Some people concentrate best in silence; for others, silence is disconcerting.

The results are what count. A child who completes assignments successfully *with* sound probably requires it as a key element of learning style. After observing a child who did her homework best with the television on, we realized that she rarely *watched* the television program—indeed, she often worked with her back to the screen. She needed sound in her learning environment and used the television for that purpose.

After you administer the Learning Style Questionnaire to your child, interpret the results; they will give you valuable knowledge of how your child learns. Additional guidelines for "reading" children's individual profiles follow the questionnaire.

The Learning Style Profile in Figure 7.2 will allow you to record your child's learning style preferences and share them with teachers. In addition to noting strong preferences, you may want to write qualitative comments in areas where they are relevant. Following the Learning Style Profile form, we have included a completed sample form for your reference (Figure 7.3). The sample is a fictitious composite of various learning style profiles.

By now, you have begun to understand how to identify and interpret learning style strengths—and how parents and teachers are able to use them as children grow and mature. If you'd like more help with interpreting the results of the Learning Style Questionnaire, refer back to Chapter 2. If you need more assistance or simply want additional information, please write to us at The Center for the Study of Learning and Teaching Styles, St. John's University, Utopia Parkway, Jamaica, New York 11439.

The Learning Style Questionnaire we've provided is aimed primarily at children in grades 3 through 12. If you have children who attend kindergarten through grade 2, a good way to discover their learning style strengths is with the *Learning Style Inventory: Primary Version* (Perrin, 1983; see Appendix B). The final chapter discusses ways in which you can help your children to guide their own learning, using your knowledge of their individual learning styles.

Figure 7.1   Learning Style Questionnaire

	True	*False*
I. *The Learning Environment*		
A. Sound		
1. I study best when it is quiet.	___	___
2. I can work with a little noise.	___	___
3. I can block out noise when I work/study.	___	___
4. Noise usually keeps me from concentrating.	___	___
5. Most of the time, I prefer to study with soft music.	___	___
6. I can work or study with any kind of music playing.	___	___
7. I like to study with rock or dance music playing.	___	___
8. Music makes it difficult for me to concentrate or study.	___	___
9. I can concentrate if people talk quietly.	___	___
10. I can study while people talk.	___	___
11. I can block out most sound when I concentrate.	___	___
12. It is difficult to block out TV sound when I concentrate.	___	___
13. Noise bothers me while I am studying.	___	___
14. Music with lyrics prevents me from studying.	___	___

Scoring Key

See whether your child answered "True" to statements 1, 4, 8, 12, 13, and 14. "True" responses to these statements are indicators that your child prefers to study and learn in quiet surroundings. If "True" was answered to four or more of those seven, your child probably will learn best in quiet situations. Conversely, if the answer was "True" for four or more of statements 2, 3, 5, 6, 7, 9, 10, and 11, your child

Figure 7.1 *(continued)*

probably works best when sound is present. If the answer was "True" to *most* of the statements, your child probably can work and learn well in either environment and has no strong preference.

	True	*False*
B. Light		
1. I like to study with lots of light.	____	____
2. I study best when the lights are low.	____	____
3. I like to read outdoors.	____	____
4. I study only for a short time if the lights are low.	____	____
5. When I study, I put all the lights on.	____	____
6. I often read or work in dim light.	____	____
7. I usually study under a shaded lamp, while the rest of the room is dim.	____	____

Scoring Key

If your child answered "True" to statements 1, 3, 4, and 5, he or she tends to work and study best in bright light. If the answer was "True" to statements 2, 6, and 7, your child learns best in low light. If six or seven statements are marked either all "True" or all "False," your child has no strong preference and lighting is not a learning style factor.

	True	*False*
C. Temperature		
1. I can concentrate if I'm warm.	____	____
2. I can concentrate if I'm cold.	____	____
3. I usually feel colder than most people.	____	____
4. I usually feel warmer than most people.	____	____
5. I like the summer.	____	____

(continued)

Figure 7.1 *(continued)*

	True	*False*
6. When it's cold outside, I like to stay indoors.	___	___
7. When it's hot outside, I like to stay indoors.	___	___
8. When it's hot outside, I go outside to play.	___	___
9. When it's cold outside, I go outside to play.	___	___
10. I find extreme heat or cold uncomfortable.	___	___
11. I like the winter.	___	___

Scoring Key

If your child answered "True" to statements 2, 4, 7, 9, and 11, he or she probably learns best in a cool environment. If the answer to statements 1, 3, 5, 6, and 8 was "True," your child learns best in a warm environment. True answers to statements 1, 2, 5, 8, 9, and 11 indicate that temperature is not an important factor in your child's learning style.

	True	*False*
D. Setting		
1. When I study, I like to sit on the floor.	___	___
2. When I study, I like to sit on a soft chair or couch.	___	___
3. When I study, I feel sleepy unless I sit on a hard chair.	___	___
4. I find it difficult to study at school.	___	___
5. I finish all my homework at home.	___	___
6. I always study for tests at home.	___	___
7. I finish all my homework in school.	___	___
8. I find it difficult to concentrate on my studies at home.	___	___

Figure 7.1 *(continued)*

	True	False
9. I work/study best in a library.	___	___
10. I can study almost anywhere.	___	___
11. I like to study in bed.	___	___
12. I like to study sitting on the carpet or a rug.	___	___
13. I can study on the floor, in a chair, on a couch, and at my desk.	___	___
14. I often study in the bathroom.	___	___

Scoring Key

If your child answered "True" to statements 3, 7, 9, and 14, he or she probably learns and studies best in a formal, traditional learning environment. A majority of "True" answers to statements 1, 2, 4, 10, 11, 12, and 14 indicates that your child prefers an informal setting for learning. "True" responses to statements 10 *and* 13 suggest that your child can learn well in either formal or informal environments. Examine *where* at home the child works if statements 5, 6, 8, or 13 were "True."

	True	False
II. *Emotional Preferences*		
A. Motivation toward schoolwork		
1. I feel good when I do well in school.	___	___
2. I feel good making my mother and father proud of me when I do well in school.	___	___
3. My teacher feels good when I do well in school.	___	___
4. Grown-ups are pleased if I bring home good reports.	___	___
5. Grown-ups are pleased when I do well in school.	___	___
6. I like making someone feel proud of me.	___	___

(continued)

Figure 7.1 *(continued)*

	True	False
7. I am embarrassed when my grades are poor.	___	___
8. It is more important to me to do well in things that happen out of school than in my schoolwork.	___	___
9. I like making my teacher proud of me.	___	___
10. Nobody really cares if I do well in school.	___	___
11. My teacher cares about me.	___	___
12. My mother cares about my grades.	___	___
13. My father cares about my grades.	___	___
14. My teacher cares about my grades.	___	___
15. Somebody cares about my grades in school.	___	___
16. I want to get good grades for myself.	___	___
17. I am happy when I do well in school.	___	___
18. I feel bad and work less when my grades are bad.	___	___
19. I feel happy and proud when my grades are good.	___	___
20. There are many things I like doing better than going to school.	___	___
21. I love to learn new things.	___	___
22. A good education will help me to get a good job.	___	___

Scoring Key

Most students tend to fall into four general categories with regard to motivation toward schoolwork; they tend to be Self-Motivated, Adult-Motivated, Teacher-Motivated, or Relatively Unmotivated. A preponderance of "True" answers to statements 1, 16, 17, 19, 21, and 22 suggests that you have a Self-Motivated child. "True" answers to statements 2, 4, 5, 6, 7, 12, 13, and 15 indicate an Adult-Motivated child. If your child is Teacher-Motivated, he or she probably answered "True" to most of statements 3, 6, 7, 9, 11, 14, and 15. "True" answers to statements 8, 10, 18, and 20 suggest that your child is Relatively Unmotivated toward schoolwork.

Figure 7.1 *(continued)*

	True	False
B. Persistence/Focus		
1. I try to finish what I start.	⎯⎯	⎯⎯
2. I usually finish what I start.	⎯⎯	⎯⎯
3. Sometimes I lose interest in things.	⎯⎯	⎯⎯
4. I rarely finish things I start.	⎯⎯	⎯⎯
5. I usually remember to finish my homework.	⎯⎯	⎯⎯
6. I often have to be reminded to do my homework.	⎯⎯	⎯⎯
7. I often forget to do or finish my homework.	⎯⎯	⎯⎯
8. I often get tired of doing things and want to start something new.	⎯⎯	⎯⎯
9. I usually like to finish things that I start.	⎯⎯	⎯⎯
10. My teacher is always telling me to finish what I'm supposed to do.	⎯⎯	⎯⎯
11. My parent(s) reminds me to finish things I have been told to do.	⎯⎯	⎯⎯
12. Other grown-ups tell me to finish things I've started.	⎯⎯	⎯⎯
13. Somebody's always reminding me to do something.	⎯⎯	⎯⎯
14. I often get tired of doing things.	⎯⎯	⎯⎯
15. I often want help in finishing things.	⎯⎯	⎯⎯
16. I like getting things done.	⎯⎯	⎯⎯
17. I like to get things done, so I can start something new.	⎯⎯	⎯⎯
18. I remember on my own to get things done.	⎯⎯	⎯⎯

(continued)

Figure 7.1 *(continued)*

Scoring Key

"True" answers to statements 1, 2, 5, 9, 16, 17, and 18 indicate that your child tends to be persistent and usually follows through and finishes tasks. "True" answers to most of statements 3, 4, 6, 8, 10, 11, 12, 13, 14, and 15 suggest that your child may be unfocused and has trouble completing tasks and projects that require persistence.

		True	*False*
C.	Responsibility/Conformity		
1.	I think I am a responsible person.	___	___
2.	People tell me that I am responsible.	___	___
3.	I always do what I promise to do.	___	___
4.	People say that I do what I said I would do.	___	___
5.	I do keep my promises most of the time.	___	___
6.	I have to be reminded over and over again to do the things I've been told to do.	___	___
7.	If my teacher tells me to do something, I try to do it.	___	___
8.	I keep forgetting to do the things I've been told to do.	___	___
9.	I usually remember to do what I'm told.	___	___
10.	People keep reminding me to do things.	___	___
11.	I like doing what I'm supposed to do.	___	___
12.	I believe that promises should be kept.	___	___
13.	I have to be reminded often to do something.	___	___

Scoring Key

"True" answers to statements 1,2, 3, 4, 5, 7, 9, 11, and 12 are an indication that your child tends to be responsible and task-oriented. "True" answers to statements 6, 8, 10, and 13 suggest that he or she may be somewhat less responsible or conforming.

Figure 7.1 *(continued)*

	True	False
D. Independence/Structure		
1. I like to be told exactly what to do.	____	____
2. I like to be able to do things in my own way.	____	____
3. I like to be given choices of how I can do things.	____	____
4. I like to be able to work things out for myself.	____	____
5. I like other people to tell me how to do things.	____	____
6. I do better if I know my work is going to be checked.	____	____
7. I do the best I can whether or not the teacher will check my work.	____	____
8. I hate working hard on something that isn't checked by the teacher.	____	____
9. I like to be given clear directions when starting new projects.	____	____

Scoring Key

If your child works and learns best in a highly supervised, structured situation, he or she probably answered "True" to most of the following statements: 1, 5, 6, 8, and 9. If you have an independent child who learns best with little supervision, he or she answered "True" to statements 2, 3, 4, and 7.

	True	False
III. *Social Needs*		
A. When I have a lot of work to do:		
1. I like to work alone.	____	____
2. I like to work with my good friend.	____	____
3. I like to work with a couple of my friends.	____	____
4. I like to work in a group of five or six classmates.	____	____

(continued)

Figure 7.1 *(continued)*

	True	False
5. I like to work with an adult.	____	____
6. I like to work with a friend but to have an adult nearby.	____	____
7. I like to work with a couple of friends but have an adult nearby.	____	____
8. I like adults nearby when I'm working alone or with a friend.	____	____
9. I like adults to stay away until my friends and I complete our work.	____	____
B. The thing I like doing best, I do:		
10. alone.	____	____
11. with a friend.	____	____
12. with a couple of friends.	____	____
13. with a group of friends.	____	____
14. with a grown-up.	____	____
15. with several grown-ups.	____	____
16. with friends and grown-ups.	____	____
17. with a member of my family who is not a grown-up.	____	____

Scoring Key

Using the following table, you can determine whether your child learns, works, and studies best alone, with same-age peers, or with adults, or demonstrates no strong preference and may work best with a combination of peers and adults. The child who works best alone, for instance, answered "True" to statements 1, 8, and 10.

Figure 7.1 *(continued)*

Statement Numbers ("True" Answers) for Social Needs Preferences					
Alone	One Peer	Two Peers	Several Peers	With Adults	With Peers and Adults
1	2	3	4	5	6
8	8	9	9	14	7
10	11	12	13	15	8
	17				16

	True	*False*

IV. *Physiological Needs*

A. Perceptual Strengths

When I learn something new, I most like to learn about it by:

1. reading about it. ___ ___

2. hearing a record. ___ ___

3. hearing a tape. ___ ___

4. seeing a filmstrip (no soundtrack). ___ ___

5. seeing and hearing a movie (with soundtrack). ___ ___

6. looking at pictures and having someone explain them. ___ ___

7. hearing my teacher tell me. ___ ___

8. playing games. ___ ___

9. going someplace and seeing for myself. ___ ___

10. having someone show me. ___ ___

(continued)

Figure 7.1 *(continued)*

	True	False

The things I remember best are the things:

11. my teacher tells me.
12. someone other than my teacher tells me.
13. someone shows me.
14. I learned about on trips.
15. I read.
16. I heard on records or tapes.
17. I heard on the radio.
18. I saw on television.
19. I read stories about.
20. I saw in a movie.
21. I tried or worked on.
22. my friends and I talked about.

I really like to:

23. read books, magazines, or newspapers.
24. see movies.
25. listen to records.
26. make tapes on a tape recorder.
27. draw or paint.
28. look at pictures.
29. play games.
30. talk to people.
31. listen to other people talk.

Figure 7.1 *(continued)*

	True	False
32. listen to the radio.	_____	_____
33. watch television.	_____	_____
34. go on trips.	_____	_____
35. learn new things with my hands.	_____	_____
36. study with friends.	_____	_____
37. build things.	_____	_____
38. do experiments.	_____	_____
39. take pictures or make movies/videos.	_____	_____
40. use typewriters, computers, calculators, or other machines.	_____	_____
41. go to the library.	_____	_____
42. trace things in substances like sand or mud.	_____	_____
43. mold things with my hands.	_____	_____

Scoring Key

This section of the questionnaire will help you to determine whether your child is primarily an Auditory, Visual, Tactile, or Kinesthetic learner.* Record the statements to which your child responded "True" in this section and compare them to the following table, to determine your child's dominant perceptual style for learning. A majority of "True" answers in any one column in the table indicates a tendency toward that perceptual style. If there is a somewhat even distribution of "True" answers through the four columns, your child probably has equally distributed perceptual style preferences.

---

*See Chapter 2 for a discussion of Auditory, Visual, Tactile, and Kinesthetic preferences.

(continued)

Figure 7.1 *(continued)*

Auditory	Visual	Tactile	Kinesthetic
Statement Numbers ("True" Answers) for Perceptual Style Preferences			
2	1	8	8
3	4	21	9
5	5	27	14
6	6	29	21
7	7	35	26
11	8	37	29
12	9	39	34
16	10	40	37
17	13	42	38
18	15	43	39
22	18		
25	19		
30	20		
31	24		
32	28		
36	33		
	41		

	True	False

B. Food Needs (Snacking, Drinking)

1. I like to eat or drink or chew while I study. ⎯⎯ ⎯⎯

2. I dislike eating, drinking, or chewing while studying. ⎯⎯ ⎯⎯

3. While I'm studying, I like to chew gum, nibble on snacks, or suck on candy. ⎯⎯ ⎯⎯

4. I can eat, drink, or nibble only after I finish studying. ⎯⎯ ⎯⎯

5. I usually eat or drink when I'm nervous or upset. ⎯⎯ ⎯⎯

6. I rarely eat when I'm nervous or upset. ⎯⎯ ⎯⎯

7. I could study better if I could eat while I'm learning. ⎯⎯ ⎯⎯

Figure 7.1 *(continued)*

	True	False
8. While I'm learning, eating something would distract me.	_____	_____
9. I often catch myself chewing on a pencil as I study.	_____	_____

Scoring Key

Some children appear to be able to concentrate and learn better if they are allowed to snack periodically while studying or working. Others are distracted by such nibbling. If your child answered "True" to statements 1, 3, 5, 7, and 9, he or she probably learns best with periodic snacks. Conversely, if most or all of statements 2, 4, 6, and 8, were answered "True," your child learns best in a food-free environment.

	True	False
C. Time		
1. I hate to get up in the morning.	_____	_____
2. I hate to go to sleep at night.	_____	_____
3. I could sleep all morning.	_____	_____
4. I stay awake for a long time after I get into bed.	_____	_____
5. I feel wide awake after 10:00 in the morning.	_____	_____
6. If I stay up very late at night I get too sleepy to remember anything.	_____	_____
7. I feel sleepy after lunch.	_____	_____
8. When I have homework to do, I like to get up early in the morning to do it.	_____	_____
9. When I can, I do my homework in the afternoon.	_____	_____
10. I usually start my homework after dinner.	_____	_____
11. I could stay up all night.	_____	_____

(continued)

Figure 7.1 *(continued)*

	True	False
12. I wish school would start near lunch time.	___	___
13. I wish I could stay home during the day and go to school at night.	___	___
14. I like going to school in the morning.	___	___
15. I can remember things when I study them:		
a. in the morning.	___	___
b. at lunchtime.	___	___
c. in the afternoon.	___	___
d. before dinner.	___	___
e. after dinner.	___	___
f. late at night.	___	___

Scoring Key

Children who answer "True" to statements 8, 14, and 15a, tend to be "morning" people; that often is the best functioning time. Those who answer "True" to statements 5, 12, and 15b, are more likely to "come alive" in late morning. However, if they answer "True" to statements 3, 5, 9, 12, 15c, and 15d, their best time of day tends to be afternoon and, if their "True" responses centered around statements 2, 4, 5, 10, 11, 13, 15e, and 15f, you have a "night owl" on your hands! A fairly equal distribution among all four categories usually indicates that the time of day or night is not an important element; that person can function equally well *when interested in what needs to be learned.*

	True	False
D. Mobility		
1. When I study, I often get up to do something (like take a drink or get a cookie) and then return to work.	___	___
2. When I study, I stay with it until I am finished and then I get up.	___	___

Figure 7.1 *(continued)*

	True	False
3. It's difficult for me to sit in one place for long.	____	____
4. I often change my position when I work and study.	____	____
5. I can sit in one place for a long time.	____	____
6. I constantly change position (or squirm) in my chair.	____	____
7. I can work best for short amounts of time with breaks in between.	____	____
8. I like getting my work done and over with quickly.	____	____
9. I like to work a little, stop, return to work, stop, return to it again, and so on.	____	____
10. I like to stick to a job and finish it.	____	____
11. I leave most jobs for the last minute and then have to work on them from beginning to end.	____	____
12. I do most of my jobs or projects a little at a time and eventually get them done.	____	____
13. I enjoy working on things without interruption when I know how to do them.	____	____

Scoring Key

If your child works and learns best in a situation in which he or she can be mobile and unfettered, the answer was probably "True" to most or all of statements 1, 3, 4, 6, 7, 9, and 12. If he or she does not require mobility and can work for long periods at one task or project without interruption or movement, the answer to most of statements 2, 5, 8, 10, 11, and 13 was probably "True." A high number of "True" and "False" answers in both columns indicates that your child has no special preference.

Figure 7.2   Learning Style Profile

Name   _____

Date   _____

Age   _____

I.   The Learning Environment

A.   Sound   _____

                    _____

B.   Light   _____

                    _____

C.   Temperature   _____

                    _____

D.   Setting   _____

                    _____

II.   Emotional Preferences

A.   Motivation   _____

                    _____

                    _____

B.   Persistence/   _____
     Focus
                    _____

                    _____

C.   Responsibility/ _____
     Conformity
                    _____

                    _____

Figure 7.2 *(continued)*

D. Independence/ _____
   Structure
                  _____

                  _____

III. Social Needs

    Appears to Learn Best:

    Alone   _____

                  _____

    With a Peer   _____

                  _____

    In a Group   _____

                  _____

    With an Adult   _____

                  _____

IV. Physiological Needs

A. Perceptual   _____
   Strengths
                  _____

B. Food Needs   _____

                  _____

C. Mobility   _____

                  _____

Figure 7.3   Sample Learning Style Profile

Name   Elizabeth Jones

Date   Jan. 12, 1992

Age   10

I.   The Learning Environment

A. Sound   Needs quiet surroundings.

B. Light   Prefers to study and work in bright light.

C. Temperature   Not important: seems to concentrate well

                       regardless of temperature.

D. Setting   Prefers a formal arrangement: conventional

                       classroom desk and chair.

II. Emotional Preferences

A. Motivation   Highly motivated academically.

B. Persistence/   Very persistent; works on tasks until completed,
    Focus   works in long attention spans.

C. Responsibility/   Extremely nonconforming; likes to do things
    Conformity   her own way.

Figure 7.3   *(continued)*

D. Independence/   Elizabeth prefers to provide her own structure;
    Structure   she is very self-structured; try to allow for
                     individuality and creativity.

III. Social Needs

    Appears to Learn Best:

    Alone   Prefers working alone. She enjoys completing
                     tasks herself.

    With a Peer   She is neither peer- nor pair-oriented.

    In a Group   No; rarely likes to work in groups. Prefers
                     independence.

    With an Adult   Prefers to work alone, but is adult-motivated
                     and wants recognition and approval from adults.

IV. Physiological Needs

A. Perceptual   Primarily visual.
    Strengths

B. Food Needs   Doesn't need to snack while studying or
                    learning.

C. Mobility   Low mobility needs; she can sit for long periods
                    of time while working on a project.

Teaching Children to Guide
Their Own Learning

Throughout this book, we have emphasized that the development of your child's giftedness depends on your identification of his or her learning style strengths, interests, and abilities. When children are encouraged to explore a variety of activities, they are likely to choose to experiment with those that stimulate their curiosity and interests. Equally important, when parents provide a nurturing support system, their child's potential is likely to emerge and develop into talents surpassing those of less advantaged children.

   We have said throughout the book that parents need to *involve* their children in many different types of activities. Gradually, and with consideration of their age and maturity, schoolchildren need to be taught how to teach themselves new and interesting material. Because young children and many adolescent males have tactual rather than visual or auditory perceptual strengths, we have suggested creating tactual materials with which they can learn.

Tactual Resources:
Why? When? For Whom?

Young children learn most easily by touching and moving objects and by engaging in activities. Although parents and teachers usually communicate with children by *speaking,* they often don't realize that most children do not become strongly auditory (likely to remember three-fourths of what they hear in a 45-minute period) until the fifth or sixth grade. Visual strength (the ability to remember three-fourths of what is seen or read in a 45-minute period) rarely develops among elementary school students before the third grade.

There are some visual or auditory children in the earlier grades, but they aren't in the majority. Even more unusual, at least one-third of high school boys remain essentially tactual (able to remember three-fourths of what they touch or manipulate) or kinesthetic (able to remember most of what they experience) and never become strongly auditory or visual. Because of the ease with which children learn tactually, instructional resources that use touch and handling should be introduced early in childhood (certainly by the third or fourth year), depending on the child's readiness and willingness to accept a hands-on learning strategy.

A cardinal rule: new and difficult material should be *introduced* through each child's perceptual strength, *reinforced* through a secondary or tertiary (but different) sense, and then *applied* by having the child use the information.

Using Information Creatively
to Increase Retention

After you introduce your child to new and difficult information through a perceptual strength and reinforce that information through a secondary or tertiary sense, your child needs to *use* what has been learned in a creative way—by applying it. After your child has learned new words or numbers, be sure they are used in any one of a variety of original ways: writing a letter to a grandparent, neighbor, or relative; writing a story; acting out an imaginary skit in which the printed words become props; illustrating and labeling the words to form a mural or painting; and so on. Chapter 6 suggests sample activities in which new information can be creatively demonstrated.

Sharing the Original Applications

After your child has invested time, effort, and energy into applying new information, any product of that personal application—a letter, story, dramatization, or game—should be corrected (if need be) and shared with others. Children need recognition for their creative efforts—giftedness emerges when a child realizes that an interest has blossomed into a skill or talent, that the talent has become productive, and that someone close, whose approval is desired, appreciates the product.

Self-motivated children often don't require extensive appreciation from others, but no child is diminished by knowing that personal efforts are praiseworthy. It is unusual for first efforts to be outstanding, but repetition ("practice makes perfect") will usually increase an ability. In addition, the entire creative process—interest plus style-directed learning plus reinforcement and application plus recognition—is likely to lead to the development of quality skills.

Nurturing Independence While Providing Support and Discipline

If children are to develop their potential and learn to teach themselves, parents must be aware of simple things they can do to foster the kind of independence that allows intellectual and aesthetic giftedness to emerge. Several examples are given here as starters.

- Allocate responsibilities to children. Assign regular household chores and acknowledge good work. Assure children that help will be there when they try things for themselves. Do *not* require everything to be done exactly as you wish; instead, provide opportunities for experimentation, for doing things differently.

- Establish a regular schedule for daily routines such as eating, sleeping, and recreation. When children are subjected to sensible regimentation, they gradually adapt to structuring their time and activities for themselves. However, some children are so self-structured that they resist schedules imposed on them by others. Be aware of your child's reactions to routines and patterns. If you encounter repeated resistance, insist on the practices that are most important to you, and permit options in other areas. Remember that each young person's learning style is different from others'. Some *want* structure and others resist and resent it. Many bright, gifted children tend to be nonconforming; imposing unnecessary structure on those children can push them into a pattern of continuous resistance. Attempt to establish routines where they are necessary (for example, the family should dine together at mealtimes), but be flexible in permitting options where appropriate.

- Listen to children's questions and look for answers to them. Don't dismiss questions as unimportant or impudent. They reflect children's curiosity and interests and are worthy of response.

- Set aside time to give each child some personal attention each day—not in a pair or a group, but individually.

Make the need for such quality time part of daily parenting in your household. Whether each parent can spare fifteen minutes a day or two hours, find the time. The fact that you and your child can be together without others intruding is extremely valuable at any age and becomes crucial as the child enters school and then moves toward and into adolescence.

- Draw out children's ideas on various subjects when you speak to them. Don't put down those you don't agree with. Instead, ask "Why do you think that's so?" or "What made you see it that way?" Listen to the responses.

- Encourage children's interest in learning, in questioning, and in thinking independently so that they will make the best possible use of gifts and abilities. Children don't have to win at everything that's tried, but should always *play* to win and always give the best possible effort.

- Arouse and sustain children's interest in a variety of activities—reading, sports, drama, music, painting, hobbies, or anything else that sparks interest, abilities, and potential. Behind each new activity is some wonderful potential that (up to this point) hasn't emerged but may well burn brightly if given the right spark. Help your child obtain a library card and take out books and tape-recorded stories before he or she learns to read. Read aloud, discuss what has been read, listen to opinions and interpretations, and ask why your child thinks something is true or not. Once a child is familiar with a story or text, encourage reading it aloud to other youngsters or adults.

- Take children to places of interest in your community and to nearby cities and towns. Take them to outdoor concerts, art exhibitions, and plays. If they can sit quietly, they are not too young to begin to enjoy indoor cultural activities. (Taking along a few nutritious snacks can pacify a small child who is caught up in the excitement of the special event, but becomes restless from sitting.)

- Pay attention to children's progress, after they enter school. Visit the school, confer with teachers, participate in parent organizations, and attend school performances. As part of your parental responsibility, become aware of current affairs and discuss them with your child. Help teachers become aware of learning style in general and your child's style in particular. Become a School Board member if you have the time.

  Remember that no method, program, or text will be effective for all children; each child learns differently. Become an advocate of *alternative* reading, science, mathematics, and social studies programs. Emphasize conducting research with new methods. Insist on parental involvement in decision making.

  Unfortunately, teachers do *not* necessarily know more than parents. Educated and informed parents who have their children's best interests at heart are likely to make better decisions for their children than will teachers who have been trained to believe that they can teach an entire classroom of schoolchildren in the same way and be equally effective for each child.

- Recognize the danger of overemphasizing grades and test scores at the expense of recreation, hobbies, and activities. Never minimize doing well in school, but defend the child's right to *choose* how time away from school is spent. A child whose potential has been awakened often spends an inordinate amount of time doing those things that are of interest, and there's no harm in that. Try to be nurturing rather than directive; provide opportunities but don't preselect their paths.

- Get help, if you don't know how to help with homework or believe your child needs more assistance than you can provide. Speak to teachers, find a mentor or a tutor. Get the homework computer disc (see page 196). *Do not permit your child to begin to fall behind in school.*

- Teach your child to respect rules made for the general good and to learn the values of discipline. Children must learn how to think for themselves and make intelligent decisions, but it's equally important that they learn to follow rules and do what is expected of them. There is a fine line between the two but, if you want to maximize your child's potential, you'll need to be conscious of tendencies in both directions.

Stimulating Children's Development

In order to teach your child how to self-teach, engage in a series of activities in which you nurture the ability to become independent. Within that focus, concentrate on developing self-discipline that understands boundaries and does not need to defy rules.

Learn when to back off and let your child express newfound talents without your hands-on participation. Once children's potential is stimulated—once they develop an interest in specific activities and then a commitment to them—they often become deeply immersed in their chosen focus. Here are some hints for when this happens.

- Try not to interrupt children who are absorbed in whatever it is they are creating, regardless of your own need for order and neatness. Let them work on their activities in a place where they can leave what they are doing and return to it later.

- Be flexible, even when coordinating everyday routines with important family activities. When your child is unusually involved in the business of creation or absorption, try to adjust mealtime or bedtime to allow for it.

- Provide whatever materials you can, to further children's interests, hobbies, or skills. Be aware of "throwaway" items that might be useful.

- Allow children to participate in making up the itinerary, when planning family trips or visits. Do some research; know precisely where you are going and what you can expect to see. Discuss the route—where you might be stopping, how long the distances between stops might be, what to look for that is of special interest. Permit choices and alternatives: "We can stop at the old mine at this town or take the train from Duquesne to Morristown—which would you prefer?"

Capitalizing on Strengths while Tackling Difficult Materials

When trying to put together one of those multipart toys children beg for before the holidays, some parents begin by reading the accompanying directions and following them from step one through to the last detail. Such people are likely to be analytic and visual; they "make sense" out of printed words. Global visuals don't pay too much attention to printed text; instead, they tend to study diagrams and illustrations, and then launch into the assembly.

Some parents rarely examine directions. They take all the parts out of the box, sort them out (according to size, shape, sequence, or color), and *then* decide what to do first. They pick items up and begin to experiment—the hands-on approach.

This usually indicates they are analytic and tactual. Their counterparts, the global/tactuals, empty the box, letting everything fall where it will, and then proceed to pick up each interesting piece—one-by-one or a handful at a time—and push, pull, jab, cajole, threaten, swear, and eventually *make* each part fit somewhere. When they have finished the task of putting the toy together, these parents often find leftover parts on the floor or table and come to realize that the gadget works quite well—maybe better—without them.

Still other parents might combine their styles and strengths: one reads the directions, the other does the hands-on assembly work, and neither cramps the other's style. Eventually, the adults get the job done. How they do it—how well they do it—depends on each parent's processing style and perceptual strength or a combination of the two.

What is true of parents is also true of children.

Applications for Highly Auditory Children

When your child's auditory scores on the Learning Style Questionnaire (see Chapter 7) are high, new and difficult material should be *heard* first, before being read or having notes taken. Here are some suggestions for auditory learners.

- Your child can listen to the teacher's lecture in class, *then* ask for the pages in the book where the information the teacher covered can be read. At home, it would be best to read the material and, at the same time, take notes or underline and answer any quiz questions the text may include. The next day, the information learned by hearing, reading, and taking notes should be converted into an original, creative, instructional resource such as a game, a play, a composition, a mural, and so on. All information should be corrected if necessary.

- Your child can read the printed information aloud onto a tape recorder, then play the tape back. Although little will be retained from an initial reading, an auditory resource will be created. Your child can then listen to the reading of the information on the tape, reread the text, and, at the same time, take notes or answer questions. The next day, what has been studied should be converted into a creative resource that can be used for reinforcement or review at a later date.

- Your child can ask a friend or classmate to read the text aloud, then read the same material quietly, take notes while reading, and convert what's been learned into a creative resource the next day.

When children are low auditory—when the auditory faculty is *not* their strength—they should begin studying new or difficult material in some other way. Their Learning Style Profile will clarify which perception is their strongest.

Applications for Highly Visual Children

- Have your child first read the text or look at charts or diagrams, then listen to the material (live or on tape) and, at the same time, take notes or illustrate the information. Auditory and tactual senses are used during the *second* exposure to the material. A follow-up should consist of making an original application of the new information to which he or she has been exposed.

- Arrange to have your child tape-record the lectures, if the teacher chooses to lecture before assigning the written material (which would help visual learners). Your child should then read the material at home, reinforce it by listening to the tape made in class, and, at the same time, take notes about what is on the tape. What has been worked on can then be applied by creating an original resource.

Applications for Highly Tactual Children

A child whose tactual scores are highest should first be exposed to new and difficult material through tactual resources. After a short exposure to such materials (alone, in a pair, or in a small group, depending on individual sociological preferences), the child should read a review of the information taught through the tactuals and, at the same time, either take notes and answer questions based on the materials or illustrate and graphically explain what is being read. The required information should then be converted into an original resource to demonstrate mastery of what must be learned. Easy-to-make, effective tactual resources are described in both 1992 Dunn and Dunn books (page 189).

Applications for Highly Kinesthetic Children

Students whose kinesthetic scores are highest should stand up, walk (within a given area), or move in place during their first exposure to new and difficult ideas—whether reading, listening, using tactual resources, or just thinking about the topic. Kinesthetic people, like joggers, often think most clearly while moving. These tips may help.

- A child whose highest scores are kinesthetic and auditory should be encouraged to stand and (quietly) move in place while listening to someone's lecture, hearing a tape recording, or viewing a videotape or movie with sound. (A combined kinesthetic and auditory preference is not common.)

- A child whose highest scores are kinesthetic and visual should read at home while walking back and forth in a familiar room. The learning can be reinforced even further by listening to the information once more (through a lecture, or a tape recording made personally by reading the book aloud) and, at the same time, taking notes or making illustrations. These steps should be followed by the development of an original resource.

Although most students can master the same knowledge and skills, *each* student should be introduced to them through his or her perceptual strength.

Teaching children to translate textbooks into resources that respond to how they (as individuals) learn is the best way teachers and parents can help schoolchildren become independent learners. Eventually, the children will be able to teach themselves anything by using the knowledge of their own learning style to translate printed matter into the instructional resource that best matches their strengths. That, however, comes at a later stage.

Capitalizing on Environmental Preferences

Children need to find a place in their environment—both at home and at school—in which each of them feels comfortable. Develop your child's awareness of sound, light, temperature, and seating design preferences and help to identify what's best in different situations.

Capitalizing on Social Preferences

After taking all of the above characteristics into account, determine whether your child learns best alone, in a pair, as part of a small group, with an adult, or in any combination of these. A child who wants to learn directly from an adult may have a preference for either an authoritative or a collegial adult. You may find that some children like to learn in a variety of ways (with frequent innovations); others may prefer patterns or routines.

Whatever the preference, we encourage you to adopt it for at least a short period of time, to determine whether your child actually performs best that way.

Capitalizing on Preferences for Food or Mobility

Children who want snacks while learning will either ask for or take them. Let your child make the decision (within your limits on *where* and *what* is permitted). Don't require your child to sit still while working. Each child learns most efficiently in his or her own way, and nagging can be as counterproductive for the young student as it is unpleasant for the nagger.

Doing Homework through Learning Style Strengths

You can use the above suggestions for capitalizing on your child's perceptual strengths, energy levels, environmental preferences, and so forth, to help with the development of good study habits. However, you must understand that the habits developed may be different from those recommended by school systems—for example, homework should be done right after school (your child may need some respite after several hours of concentration); or, a child should work at a desk and chair in a quiet room under a bright light (these may not be your child's preferences for learning).

In Chapter 2, we discussed research that demonstrates the importance of encouraging children to capitalize on their learning style strengths. A particular way to study is great for some students and absolutely counterproductive for others. Test your child, to identify his or her learning style, then use the style to bring out your child's potential and get homework done effectively.

When you know your child's strengths, you can utilize a particular approach for each type of perception. Here are some suggestions for *instructions* to give your child.

- *Visual* child—Ask the teacher which pages in the book can be read at home each night *before* a lecture on a new, difficult topic. Do the reading, then take notes while listening to the teacher's lecture or the class discussion of the new lesson.

- *Auditory* child—Listen carefully in school, then read and take notes from the printed material when at home.

- *Tactual* child—Convert all the important information in the book to tactual items. Then read the text and take notes.

- *Kinesthetic* child—Walk, rock in a chair, or *move* while reading, writing, or listening (whichever is the next strongest faculty after kinesthetic). Then, reinforce the material in two other ways (the third and fourth strongest faculties), to remember and be able to apply the information. (Many kinesthetic children need real-life experiences in supermarkets, museums, and so forth, to learn.)

Add the other ingredients of style—time, the environment, and so forth—and you will likely find your child boasting that schoolwork isn't really all that hard.

Teaching Children How to Take Tests

Test taking can become stressful for many students who, for different reasons, become "brain dead" just before an examination and remain that way until the moment their teacher begins collecting the papers. There are many helpful hints children can use to improve performance and reduce tension while taking exams. Here are just a few of them.

- Many IQ and achievement tests direct students to "read the following passage and then answer the questions that follow." When students do that, they don't necessarily know what to read *for*. They get to the end of the passage, read the questions, and then have to reread the material to find answers. Tell your child to skip over these instructions, read the questions at the end of the passage first, and *then* read the passage and answer the questions.

  After this procedure becomes comfortable, tell your child that almost all test makers are analytics: they devise one question at a time, based on the text, and the questions appear in the exact sequence of the information presented. As the questions at the end of the passage are read (before actually reading the passage itself), your child should concentrate on the first two or three questions and read for those answers. Chances are good that the answers will be found in the exact sequence in which the questions are posed. When that doesn't happen, it's best to skip over what can't be found, continue to the end, and, after completing all the questions that can be answered easily, go back and work on the questions that seem most difficult.

- Any questions that seem really hard should be bypassed. Your child should complete all the easier ones, *then* go back and work on the more elusive ones.

- The comprehension questions are generally posed at the end of a sequence, unless the question is something like "What would be the best title for this story?" In that case, your child should ask "What is this reading really all about?" That should help in focusing on the topic.

- Before the test-taking years begin, emphasize that all anyone can do on a test is give a best effort. When that has been done, there's no reason to be concerned or distressed. Help your child develop the habit of studying for a test several times during the week before the test is given, but make it clear that a wholehearted attempt to master the material is all that is expected.

  Try to reduce test-taking stress for your child. Many children don't function well under tension; others only do well when they get themselves "hyped" for a test. Help your child relax before the test and, if anxiety persists, give reassurance that, because of all the hard studying for the test, *you* feel confidence in his or her ability to do well.

- Consider your child's learning style, and help with preparations for the actual test taking that will allow functioning more easily while answering the questions. Provide healthful snacks, a warm sweater, a lamp, or a seat cushion—whatever will help.

Developing Self-Teaching Strategies for Unique Children

There are no specific rules that will always apply to gifted children, but there is a general principle: if you help them develop their best potential, they will shine in everything they do that's important to them. Some authorities may tell you otherwise, but remember that even professionally trained, certified experts have made mistakes in both child rearing and education. Every time that any specific method, practice, resource, or program is suggested as being effective for all—or even most—children, ignorance is demonstrated. Children are like snowflakes: each is unique, special, and vulnerable.

Use your own best instincts, add your experiential knowledge of your child's learning style, and filter your knowledge through this book's information concerning giftedness: the whole package is your guide. Your gut reaction will have to be the determining factor. Bright children are different from average children and vastly different from underachievers, but they also are very different from each other. True, they have many characteristics in common, but they also have many that are theirs alone.

Never forget that bright children share some characteristics with underachievers: most want love, caring, and nurturing; they want to be part of a family, to do well, to have time for the things that interest them most, to be safe from harm, and so on. Had many underachievers' potentials been nurtured, they probably would have achieved more.

A case in point involved children attending the Brightwood Elementary School in Greensboro, North Carolina. In July 1986, the school reported reading and mathematics scores in the 30th percentile. In an attempt to improve those scores, the principal, Roland Andrews, came to New York to study at St. John's University's Learning Styles Leadership Institute for one week. The next year (1987), Brightwood's scores on the same standardized test (the California Achievement Test or CAT) rose to the 40th percentile. Most of Brightwood's lower-middle-class, black parents were so impressed with the improvement in their children's achievement and attitudes that they contributed funds to send five more teachers to St. John's the next summer.

In 1988, Brightwood's children scored between the 74th and 77th percentile in reading and math, and its minority children scored *21 percent above* the state's average for all children, black and white. By 1989, Brightwood's CAT scores reached the 83rd percentile. Thus, between 1986 and 1989, those same children showed between 15 and 21 percent improved achievement each year over their previous test scores— and the only thing teachers did differently during that three-year period was to introduce learning-style-based instruction.

The system used at Brightwood included:

1. Identifying children's learning styles.

2. Telling each child what his or her strengths were.

3. Starting instruction tactually, kinesthetically, and globally for those who were essentially tactual/kinesthetic/global.

4. Redesigning classrooms to respond to the children's needs for music or background noise, soft light, and informal seating.

5. Substituting many short assignments for a few long ones.

6. Recognizing that classmates' styles differed and individuals had the privilege of capitalizing on their strengths (so long as their methods did not distract students with different styles).

7. Being taught how to study and do homework through individual prescriptions (generated by the St. John's University computer software, designed specifically for that purpose).

Many schools have made similarly impressive gains by changing instructional methods to make them responsive to individuals' learning style strengths. Think for a moment: if underachieving students have been able to break their pattern and become normally achieving, imagine what responsiveness to students' strengths could do if it began at the start of their education, when they are young and impressionable.

In schools with high-achieving populations, learners in grades 2 through 12 have been taught to translate their textbooks into Contract Activity Packages, Programmed Learning Sequences, and high-interest independent studies. Students who become interested in any specialty—reading, math, science, art, music, social studies, drama, sports, sculpture, dance, building, modeling, opera, theater, poetry, computers, foreign language, and people-oriented activities—can teach themselves anything, once their potential has been stimulated.

Parents and teachers must *permit* their children and students to find and make those learning choices. Throughout this book, we have recommended that you provide a strong support system for your child, beginning in infancy and continuing throughout young adult years. Now comes an addendum: parents must anticipate that gifted children can and will want to teach themselves. When they do, their parents must learn to let go.

Don't expect your child to be outstanding in every field, or even in many endeavors. Outstanding accomplishments are hard to come by, and equity demands that no one monopolize all learning potentials, but that virtually all children have some. Permit your child to develop his or her potentials, and allow choices as to how (and how much) those will be nurtured. Don't *ever* say "How can you be so bright in [one field] and so stupid in [another]?" Your child may be one age chronologically, another developmentally, another emotionally, another psychologically, and still another in terms of giftedness. No one excels in everything. Admit it: *even you,* as a student and now as a parent, probably didn't make the most of your own potentials. Give your child a break; don't aim too high.

Don't compare your child with any other child. It's not only unfair to both, but many children feel the burden of being "best" or "better" much of the time. No one should have to bear that burden. Even without parental pressure, many gifted children withdraw from competition or academics because they don't want to always have to be better than—or even just unlike—other children. Acknowledge to your child that he or she has gifts in certain areas, and that those are appreciated. At the same time, acknowledge that *many* children are gifted, in many different ways, and that every child is special because every human being is special.

Don't overschedule your child. Make the most of childhood years, the time to be a child and to play, daydream, relax, and be goofy and uninvolved at times. Thinking can be done anywhere at any time, but people need to do it in their own way.

Don't expect that giftedness can be developed without problems; it often requires a great deal of parental time, effort, devotion, and blind adoration. Your child's gifts are a blessing, but even blessings can sometimes be a problem. Enjoy children for what they are—not for what you dreamed they would be.

Praise and encourage your child for his or her talents and efforts—for trying to be outstanding in a special area, for succeeding, and for risking failure and sometimes experiencing it. Encourage continuing effort, especially when things go wrong. Develop the feeling that the fun is in the trying; winning may be sweet but the courage, energy, and risk-taking effort are what really count most.

Anticipate being asked odd questions and being exposed to strange, new ideas. In whichever area they excel, productive people think and do things differently—precisely because they *are* unique and they enjoy unusual insights and perspectives. Don't ever ridicule their thoughts; consider them and accept them. Instead of "That's silly," try "I never thought of it quite like that" or "What makes you think that?" In addition, *really listen* to the things your child says. All children cease to ask questions and share ideas if no one pays attention or if their thoughts are disparaged. They are thinking, and *that* is what is important. Encourage that process; don't stifle it.

Parents can do many things to provide an environment and climate in which independent thinking and teaching can occur. No one can do *everything;* don't feel as if you have to. Every suggested step you take will increase your child's chances for critical thinking, problem solving, and self-teaching. Do as much as you can, and feel good about having tried.

In Closing . . .

At the turn of the century, the French psychologist Alfred Binet sought to measure intelligence through puzzle-like problems. The system he created has endured until today. Either we ask students to remember an inordinate amount of extraneous detail (often unrelated to their lives and interests) and then pit them against their peers to see who can recall the most, or we ask them to solve problems that often are esoteric and fragmented (*train* is to *track* as *boat* is to _____). The ability to figure out such relationships *is* one form of intelligence, and some people are extremely gifted in this way. But problem solving and rote memory put together are not the whole of intelligence.

Schools often ignore—or even relegate to failure—students with other, more creative kinds of intelligence. Consider those who have the ability to originate beautiful music, art, dance, drama, photography, prose, and philosophy, or a talent for design, mechanics, electrical innovations, architecture, or needlework. Wherever there is humanity, we need people who have the sensitivity to reach and energize human beings, provide leadership under stress and heroics in dangerous situations, and galvanize courage when only despair is evident; to value humanity and uplift people's spirits; to provide direction and seek solutions when none is apparent; to explore new paths and move forward on roads that others fear to tread; to produce poetry that inspires and revitalizes, clothing that enhances the stature of modest persons, products that cure illness and provide safety and security for masses.

Why certain human talents and gifts become respected and others do not is difficult to explain. All gifts enhance the quality of life; all talent enriches those whom it touches; all beauty adds to our pleasure; all ability is valuable. In the United States, talents that produce monetary wealth seem to be more highly valued than others; in other parts of the world, age, prestige, heritage, or beauty are valued more. We damage our children, ourselves, and society when we restrict recognition of giftedness to verbal or mathematical ability and exclude from stature the many other forms of giftedness that uplift individuals and all those with whom they interact.

More critical than the lack of recognition of various forms of talent are the experiences that many educators know by heart: the child of neglect and deprivation who suddenly, through a single exposure, develops a love for something, exerts energies in a single direction, and masters the skills necessary to reach national or international recognition as being among the most gifted in that field. The potential was there, but nothing helped to release it until that one fortuitous moment or incident.

Thousands of such stories are on record; they are more common than psychologists and educators are willing to admit. The fourth-grade girl whose poem the teacher praised and read to the class . . . who became a published writer. The adolescent who failed in school and played hookey to spend hours in the family garage "tinkering" with gadgets . . . who eventually invented the Apple computer. The near-deaf boy who would not give up his obsession to devise a "box that could talk" . . . who eventually designed the telephone. The preoccupied schoolboy who had trouble with math . . . who developed the Theory of Relativity. The "madman" who thought the earth was round . . . who eventually proved that the entire world was wrong and he was correct.

Giftedness is not a single trait. It is an explosion of dormant potential that somehow emerges and inspires its owner to form an interest, which leads to a commitment, which leads to a devotion, which leads to a love. A gift, in defiance of everyone else's beliefs, captures the heart and soul of a human being who then is willing to devote time, energy, and talent to its full fruition. Whereas human beings cannot *create* giftedness, they certainly can help unlock the door to permit individual potential to emerge. The emergence may come quietly, and few notice; but sometimes it bursts forth and everyone becomes aware.

Some people have many kinds of giftedness; some have only one or two. But we contend that almost every individual has the *potential* to be gifted. In the right set of circumstances, that gift or talent *will* be realized. We cannot choose our children's gifts; we can only provide a healthy environment in which abilities and talents emerge and can then be fostered.

In recent years, misuse of IQ tests and other psychological instruments has been challenged in many quarters. As we indicated earlier, both IQ and standard achievement tests measure only narrow ranges and types of giftedness. Talents that are not revealed by those tests may exist within the individual but, because they have not been sufficiently nurtured, they might never emerge. Even more serious, the multiple kinds of gifts that children possess often are ignored or quashed in school ("Stop singing to yourself!," "Walk, don't *dance,* in the halls!," "Stop drawing in your notebook!," "Don't play with those gadgets! You are here to learn!," or "All you ever do is talk to Mary! Can't you concentrate on anything serious?")

Senator Bill Bradley of New Jersey, the former New York Knick basketball star, was also a Princeton graduate and a Rhodes scholar, but that combination of outstanding intellect and athletic ability is rare. A much more common expectation is that well-known athletes will have a difficult time passing academic subjects—not because they are not sufficiently intelligent, but because their giftedness is tactual/kinesthetic, featuring high mobility strengths. Most academic disciplines (and most teachers) require auditory or visual passivity, which is the very *opposite* of athletes' learning style. If athletes were taught in a way that fit their learning style, they could easily improve, as did the students in the Brightwood school.

Unfortunately, most teachers are trained to teach essentially one way (although they universally deny it): through lectures and classroom discussions, which are *auditory*. When students do not learn that way, they are required to read the materials, which are *visual*. Teachers are rarely taught or permitted to teach tactually and kinesthetically. They may do it as a last resort, *after* they have exhausted the basic auditory and visual strategies (and made the students feel that the work is too difficult and beyond their abilities). Even then, manipulative teaching techniques usually follow auditory or visual instruction.

In our experience, schools that have implemented instructional programs based on learning styles have consistently shown good results: they report significantly increased achievement among previously failing students. That could never have happened if the potential for achievement had not existed. The potential was *always* there; the schools had never before tapped into it. We hope that more and more educators will experiment with learning styles and find better ways to reach more children.

But this book is primarily for laypeople, for parents. We want *you* to take the initiative in finding the giftedness in your child and experiencing the joy, in yourself and in your child, of its discovery and fulfillment.

Appendices

Appendix A

Further Reading

Learning Styles

Annotated Bibliography on Learning Styles. (1991). Jamaica, NY: St. John's University Center for the Study of Learning and Teaching Styles.

Dunn, R., and Dunn, K. (1977). *Administrator's Guide to New Programs for Faculty Management and Evaluation.* Englewood Cliffs, NJ: Prentice-Hall.

———. (1978). *Teaching Students Through Their Individual Learning Styles: A Practical Approach.* Englewood Cliffs, NJ: Prentice-Hall.

———. (1986). *Teaching Students to Read Through Their Individual Learning Styles.* Englewood Cliffs, NJ: Prentice-Hall.

———. (1992). *Teaching Elementary Students Through Their Individual Learning Styles.* Boston: Allyn & Bacon.

———. (1992). *Teaching Secondary Students Through Their Individual Learning Styles.* Boston: Allyn & Bacon.

Dunn, R., and Griggs, S. A. (1988). *Learning Styles: Quiet Revolution in American Secondary Schools.* Reston, VA: National Association of Secondary School Principals.

Griggs, S. A. (1991). *Learning Styles Counseling.* Jamaica, NY: St. John's University Center for the Study of Learning and Teaching Styles.

Learning Styles Network Newsletter (1979—). Jamaica, NY: National Association of Secondary School Principals and St. John's University (cosponsors).

Giftedness and Creativity

Davis, G. A., and Rimm, S. B. (1989). *Education of the Gifted and Talented*, 2d edition. Englewood Cliffs, NJ: Prentice-Hall.

Eberle, B., and Stanish, B. (1985). *CPS for Kids.* East Aurora, NY: DOK Publishers.

Milgram, R. A. (Ed.). (1989). *Teaching Gifted and Talented Students in the Regular Classroom.* Springfield, IL: Charles C Thomas.

Shallcross, D. J. (1981). *Teaching Creative Behavior.* Englewood Cliffs, NJ: Prentice-Hall.

Smith, J. M. *Setting Conditions for Creative Teaching in the Elementary School.* Boston: Allyn & Bacon.

Treffinger, D. J., Isaksen, S. G., and Firestien, R. L. (1982). *Handbook of Creative Learning.* Volume 1. Williamsville, NY: Center for Creative Learning.

Treffinger, D. J. (1983). "Methods, techniques, and educational programs for stimulating creativity." In A. J. Tanenbaum (Ed.), *Gifted Children: Psychological and Educational Perspectives.* New York: Macmillan.

Van Oech, R. (1983). *A Whack in the Side of the Head.* New York: Warner Books.

Parenting

Bempechat, J., and Wells, A. S. (1989). "Promoting the achievement of at-risk students." *Trends and Issues,* No. 13. New York: ERIC Clearinghouse on Urban Education, Teachers College, Columbia University.

Bempechat, J. (1990). "The role of parent involvement in children's academic achievement: A review of the literature." *Trends and Issues,* No. 14. New York: ERIC Clearinghouse on Urban Education, Teachers College, Columbia University.

Bloom, B. (1985). *Developing Talent in Young People.* New York: Ballantine Books.

Dunn, R., and Dunn, K. (1977). *How to Raise Independent and Professionally Successful Daughters.* Englewood Cliffs, NJ: Prentice-Hall.

Epstein, J. (1987). "Toward a theory of family–school connections: Teacher practices and parent involvement." In K. Kurrelmann, F. Kaufman, and F. Lasel (Eds.), *Social Intervention: Potential and Constraints.* New York: De Gruyter.

Henderson, R. (1981). "Home environment and intellectual performance." In R. Henderson (Ed.), *Parent–Child Interaction: Theory, Research, and Prospects.* New York: Academic Press.

Holloway, S., and Hess, R. (1985). "Mothers' and teachers' attributions about childrens' mathematics performance." In I. Sigel (Ed.), *Parent Belief Systems.* Hillsdale, NJ: Erbaum.

McGillicuddy-DeLisi, A., DeLisi, R., Flaugher, J., and Sigel, I. (1986). "Familial influences on planning." In J. Kagan (Ed.), *Blueprints for Thinking.* Cambridge: Cambridge University Press.

Olmstead, P., and Rubin, R. (1983). "Parent involvement: Perspectives from the Follow-Through Experience." In R. Haskins and D. Adams (Eds.), *Parent Education and Public Policy.* Norwood, NJ: Ablex.

White, Burton. (1986). *The First Years of Life,* 3d edition. Englewood Cliffs, NJ: Prentice-Hall.

Appendix *B*

Instruments for Diagnosing Learning Styles of Various Age Groups

Dunn, R., Dunn, K., and Price, G. E. (1989 latest). *Productivity Environmental Preference Survey (PEPS): An Instrument for Identifying the Learning Style Strength of Adults.* Available from Price Systems, Box 1818, Lawrence, KS 66044.

————. (1989 latest). *Learning Style Inventory (LSI): An Instrument for Identifying the Learning Style Strengths of Students in Grades 3–12.* Available from Price Systems, Box 1818, Lawrence, KS 66044.

Perrin, J. (1983). *Learning Style Inventory: Primary Version (LSI:P): An Instrument for Identifying the Learning Styles of Children in Grades K–2.* Available from The Center for the Study of Learning and Teaching Styles, St. John's University, Utopia Parkway, Jamaica, NY 11439.

Appendix C

Additional Resources for Capitalizing on Individual Learning Styles

The following materials, especially developed for use with students in different grade levels, are available from The Center for the Study of Learning and Teaching Styles, St. John's University, Utopia Parkway, Jamaica, NY 11439.

Storybooks for Children

Elephant Style, by Janet Perrin and Stephanie Santore. An excellent resource with which to prepare primary children to take a learning styles assessment. It explains the concept of learning style through the saga of Ellie and Phonty, two elephants who do everything together—but they can't learn the same things in the same way at school. The book walks children through many of the elements of style through a playful picture story.

Mission from No Style, by Ann Braio. A delightful saga that explains the concept of learning style to students in grades 2 to 6. Space children are searching for guidelines concerning how to learn new and difficult information. Earthlings join them, and eventually unravel how to do well in school. This high-interest tale should be read to children *before* diagnosing learning style, to seed an understanding that everyone has different strengths.

Two-of-a-Kind Learning Styles, by Rosy Pena. A sensitive story that simultaneously explains learning style and develops an understanding of individual differences among middle-school adolescents. Through a series of escapades, Global Myrna and Analytic Victor, close friends who enjoy being together while relaxing, find that they cannot do their homework together. They learn to respect their individual characteristics and study difficult material through their own unique learning style strengths.

The Global / Analytic Coloring Book, by Sr. Miriam Lenihan. A sister-and-brother story that gradually reveals how to know whether you are global or analytic, and then how to use your strengths to your advantage while learning.

Vive La Difference: Guide Explaining Learning Style to High School Students, by Connie Bowman. Written specifically for high school students.

Homework Prescriptions Based on Learning Style Strengths

Learning How to Learn Homework through Style (computer disc). A software package that provides students in grades 3–12 with individual prescriptions for doing their homework and studying in ways that complement their personal learning styles. Because students are taught how to work through their strengths, they find doing homework less stressful and more productive. This computer disc is available in IBM and Apple. It works only with Learning Style Inventory data and, thus, requires prior testing with that diagnostic instrument.

Resources for Parents

Learning How to Be Productive through Adult Style (computer disc). A software package that provides adults with individual prescriptions for concentrating and producing in ways that complement their personal learning styles. Because adults are shown how to work through their strengths, being productive is less stressful and more effective. This disc is available in IBM and Apple. It works only with *Productivity Environmental Preference Survey* data, and thus requires prior testing with that diagnostic instrument.

Learning Styles: An Explanation for Parents. A filmstrip and videotape explaining the concept of learning style.

Learning Styles: A Guide For Parents, by Sr. Natalie Lafser. A booklet that explains learning style as it relates to parents and provides a printed account of how parents can accommodate their children's learning styles at home.

Learning Styles Counseling, by Shirley A. Griggs. A comprehensive book describing how to reach troubled or confused individuals through their learning styles. Although written specifically for counselors, it also should be read by parents and teachers.

Personal Learning Power, by Kenneth Dunn. A rap video by high school students who, through song and dance, explain learning styles (for grades 3–12 and adults).

Appendix *D*

Organizations Concerned with Learning Styles

United States

(The) Association for the Gifted (TAG)
Council for Exceptional Children
1920 Association Drive
Reston, VA 22091

Center for Slow Learners
Carole Marshall, Assistant Director
1122 North Adams, Suite #220
Richardson, TX 75081

Center for the Study of Learning and Teaching Styles and
    National Network Learning Styles Center
Professor Rita Dunn, Director
St. John's University
Utopia Parkway
Jamaica, NY 11439

Erie 1 Boces Learning Styles Division
Instructional Development Center
Carolyn Brunner, Director
Terrace Education Center
591 Terrace Boulevard
Depew, NY 14043

Learning Styles Network
Association for Supervision and Curriculum Development
1250 North Pitt Street
Alexandria, VA 22314
Attn: Dr. Helene Hodges

National Association for Gifted Children
1155 15th Street NW, Suite 1002
Washington, DC 20005

National Learning Styles Network Center
Dr. Katy Lux, Director
Aquinas College
Grand Rapids, MI 49506

National Learning Styles Network Center
Dr. Joseph L. Vaughan, Director
Department of Elementary Education
East Texas State University
East Texas Station
Commerce, TX 75428

National Learning Styles Network Center
Dr. Barbara Given, Director
George Mason University
4400 University Drive
Fairfax, VA 22030

National Learning Styles Network Center
National Association of Secondary School Principals
Dr. James W. Keefe, Director of Research
1904 Association Drive
Reston, VA 22091

Office of Learning Styles, St. Louis Archdiocese
Natalie Lafser, C. S. J., Director
3500 St. Catherine Street
Florissant, MO 63033

Price Systems
Box 1818
Lawrence, KS 66044

Canada

Learning Center
Betty-Ann Kuhn, Director
938 Huntleigh Crescent
Kamloops, British Columbia, Canada V1S 1H1

Learning Styles Assistance for Elementary School Special
    Education Students
Glenna Mae Lawton and Kenneth Lawton, Co-Directors
Box 62
Manilla, Ontario, Canada K0M 2J0

Learning Styles: The Canadian Connection
Phyllis Elfan and Barbara Worden, Directors
134 Aspenwood Drive
Willowdale, Ontario, Canada M2H 2G1

Learning Styles School Specialist
Anne Reid, Teacher, Princess Margaret Public Schools
51 Wellington Street
Orangeville, Ontario L9W 216

Index